Henry Solon Graves

Practical Forestry in the Adirondacks

Henry Solon Graves

Practical Forestry in the Adirondacks

ISBN/EAN: 9783337182557

Printed in Europe, USA, Canada, Australia, Japan

Cover: Foto ©Andreas Hilbeck / pixelio.de

More available books at **www.hansebooks.com**

BULLETIN No. 26.

U. S. DEPARTMENT OF AGRICULTURE.

DIVISION OF FORESTRY.

GIFFORD PINCHOT, FORESTER.

PRACTICAL FORESTRY

IN

THE ADIRONDACKS.

BY

HENRY S. GRAVES,
SUPERINTENDENT OF WORKING PLANS.

WASHINGTON:
GOVERNMENT PRINTING OFFICE.
OCTOBER, 1899.

LETTER OF TRANSMITTAL.

U. S. DEPARTMENT OF AGRICULTURE,
DIVISION OF FORESTRY,
Washington, D. C., July 8, 1899.

SIR: I have the honor to transmit herewith a report entitled Practical Forestry in the Adirondacks, by Henry S. Graves, superintendent of working plans in the Division of Forestry, and to recommend its publication as Bulletin No. 26 of this Division.

In addition to an account of the general conditions which govern forest management in the Adirondacks, this report contains a statement of work done and results accomplished in that region under the provisions of Circular No. 21 of the Division of Forestry. In this circular, under date of October 8, 1898, the Department offered to assist farmers, lumbermen, and others in handling their forest lands. The response was immediate and widespread. Requests for such assistance have been received for about one and one-half million acres of forest land, approximately 400,000 acres of which have already received attention. Of the latter, the two tracts dealt with in this bulletin form a most important part. So far as the Division is informed one of the tracts, of an area of 68,000 acres, supplies the first instance of the practice of systematic forestry by a lumber company in the Adirondacks, and by far the most extensive example of forest management in the United States. The other tract, Nehasane Park, though smaller, is of peculiar interest, because its conditions are exceptionally favorable for forest management and because the methods of lumbering upon it are being rapidly improved.

It is shown in the report that the first year's work on the above-mentioned tracts was in some respects unsatisfactory, but that, under the circumstances, the high class of lumbering which is being done during the present season could not have been expected until the new methods had been tried and the woodsmen had had experience in them. Any attempt violently to overturn established ways of doing work in the woods must fail. Methods consecrated by years of practice yield slowly to the changes advocated by the Division, but still they yield. The first year's work in the Adirondacks under the provisions of Circular No. 21, although it secured the safety and reproduction of the forest, was rough. It is a matter for congratulation that the second year's lumbering is beginning under much better conditions and with the promise of great improvement in the character of the work.

Respectfully,

GIFFORD PINCHOT, *Forester.*

Hon. J. H. BRIGHAM,
Acting Secretary.

3

CONTENTS.

6 CONTENTS.

ILLUSTRATIONS.

PRACTICAL FORESTRY IN THE ADIRONDACKS.

INTRODUCTION.

It has long been apparent that the methods of forestry will not find general acceptance among owners of woodland until it has been shown by actual trial that they are practicable and profitable. In order to provide a series of examples of forest management in different sections of the United States, the Department of Agriculture offered in Circular No. 21, Division of Forestry, issued in October, 1898, to give practical assistance to farmers, lumbermen, and others in handling forest lands. This offer was that the Division of Forestry would make a personal study of a limited number of tracts which seemed to present favorable opportunities to illustrate forest management, and, should it appear advisable after a preliminary examination, would prepare plans for the forest work and supervise their execution. No charge was to be made for the work in case of tracts under 200 acres, nor for the preliminary examination of larger areas; but owners of large tracts were expected to defray the traveling expenses of the agent or agents of the Division while engaged in preparing working plans and in the work of carrying them out, and to furnish such assistance as was necessary.

The conditions upon which the Division proposed to cooperate with owners of timber land are stated in the following agreement with Dr. W. S. Webb, the owner of Nehasane Park, one of the tracts considered in this report:

TIMBER-LAND AGREEMENT.

WASHINGTON, D. C., June 15, 1899.

The Department of Agriculture of the United States and W. S. Webb, of New York, county of New York, State of New York, mutually agree together as follows:

1. The Department of Agriculture, in pursuance of investigations in forestry, and in order to disseminate a knowledge of improved ways of handling forest lands, shall, after personal study on the ground by its agent or agents, prepare a plan for harvesting the forest crop and reproducing the forest on the land of the said W. S. Webb, situated and described as follows: 40,000 acres, more or less, of virgin forest land in townships 37 and 38, county of Hamilton, and townships 42 and 43, county of Herkimer, State of New York.

2. The said plan shall be prepared for the purpose of promoting and increasing the present value and usefulness of the said land to its owner, and to perpetuate and improve the forest upon it.

3. Upon the completion of the said plan and its acceptance by the said W. S. Webb, the Department of Agriculture shall supervise the execution thereof so far as may be necessary.

9

4. The cost of executing the provisions of this agreement shall be paid as follows:

(a) The salaries of all the employees of the Department of Agriculture engaged in fulfilling this agreement shall be paid by the Department.

(b) A preliminary visit of inspection, if required, shall be wholly at the charge of the Department.

(c) Actual and necessary expenses for travel and subsistence of the agent or agents of the Department working under this agreement, except as provided in the foregoing paragraph (b), shall be paid by the said W. S. Webb. What are "actual and necessary expenses" shall be determined by the printed regulations of the Department. Expenses under this paragraph (c) are estimated, for the preparation of this working plan, at ——— dollars.

(d) Necessary assistants shall be furnished by the said W. S. Webb without cost to the Department. It is estimated that ——— such assistants will be required for ——— months to prepare this working plan.

(e) The Department shall not participate in any degree in the receipts and expenses arising from said land, except as above provided.

5. The Department of Agriculture shall have the right to publish and distribute the said plan and its results for the information of lumbermen, forest owners, and others whom it may concern.

6. This agreement may be dissolved by either party upon ten days' notice given to the other.

     (Signed)   JAMES WILSON.

     (Signed)   ——— ———.

WASHINGTON, D. C., June 15, 1899.

The working plan above mentioned being now completed is accepted, and will be carried out under the conditions and during the validity of the above agreement.

     (Signed)   W. S. WEBB.

The form of agreement with owners of small wood lots is similar to the above, except that the expenses incurred in the preparation of the working plans and in supervising their execution are borne entirely by the Department of Agriculture.

Previous to the publication of Circular No. 21, in October, 1898, it became known among a number of landowners that an offer of assistance was to be made, and, in anticipation, eight applications were sent in during the summer. Among these were applications from Dr. W. S. Webb for a tract of 40,000 acres in the Adirondacks and from Hon. W. C. Whitney for an adjoining tract of 68,000 acres. The forest work was organized on these lands without delay. On the former no preliminary work was necessary, for during the previous year a complete working plan, which was subsequently published in "The Adirondack Spruce," by Gifford Pinchot, had been prepared. On account of the similarity of conditions between the two tracts it was found that this working plan could also be applied in its main features to the Whitney Preserve. It was only necessary, therefore, to make a rapid examination of the latter tract, which was completed by the writer in September, 1898.

A full account of the work done on the two preserves is given in the present report. The writer has endeavored to state not only the points

---

During 1897 a complete working plan was made for Nehasane Park, so that under this paragraph no expense will be involved.

in which the work of forestry proved a complete success, but also how
the first year's lumbering was in certain respects unsatisfactory. (Pl. II.)
At the writing of this report the second year's work has already been
begun under the most favorable circumstances and with every indication that the lumbering will be carried on to the entire satisfaction of
the owners and of the Forester of the Department of Agriculture.

In the first part of the report the problem of forestry in the Adirondacks is discussed in detail, with special reference to the two private
preserves under consideration. There follows, then, a description of
these tracts and of the forest growing on them, and a special study of
the habits, growth, and production of the Spruce, with brief mention
of the associated species. In connection with the special working plan
for the preserves, given in the latter part of the report, the loss occasioned by ordinary lumbering is discussed in detail, to show the
advantage of conservative methods.

The majority of the tables in the report and a portion of the descrip-
tive matter, dealing with the sylvicultural character, growth, and production of the Spruce, have been largely taken from "The Adirondack
Spruce," with the author's permission. This book contains the results
of a study of the Spruce, together with a working plan for Nehasane
Park, made in 1897 in cooperation with Dr. W. S. Webb, the owner of
the land. The work of collecting the data in the field for the above-
mentioned study was carried on under the supervision of the writer.

The portions of the report compiled from "The Adirondack Spruce"
are as follows: "Nehasane Park," page 21; "Special consideration of
the Spruce," page 32; "Birch," "Beech," "Hard Maple," "Hemlock,"
"Balsam," "Soft Maple," pages 51 to 53; "The growth of Spruce," page
39; "Yield tables," page 46; "Application of the yield tables," page 48,
and "Volume tables," page 78.   All of the tables in the report have
been quoted except those found on pages 33, 47, 48, 58, and 60.

AN AMERICAN SYSTEM OF FORESTRY.

During the past few years a widespread interest in forest problems
has been aroused throughout the United States. This is indicated by
the establishment of new forest reserves in the West, the formation of
forest associations, the enactment of vigorous laws in a number of
the States, the efforts of private individuals toward Federal and State
legislation, and the favorable attitude of the press. Yet, in spite of
this interest, there still remains a strong impression among very many
business men that methods of forestry can be used only by the State
or by wealthy landowners, to whom the preservation of the forest
is the first and the money return is a secondary consideration. The
existence of this feeling is proved by the fact that until the past year
there have been practically no experiments in systematic forest management on a large scale except by a few wealthy men. This is partly

due to utter indifference toward the subject, but more particularly to a misunderstanding of the scope of forestry and the methods advocated by the forester.

In continental Europe the forests have been under careful modern management for over a century, and very thorough methods have been developed. It has been natural in advocating the practice of forestry in this country to cite the example of Europe, and to describe the systems there employed. The details of method have, however, been made more prominent than broad principles, and many have been led to believe that, unless these methods are adopted, forestry can not be practiced at all.

The systems of forestry employed in Europe are the result of years of study and experiment, and have been developed along certain lines in obedience to local economic conditions. We may profit from this experience through having an object lesson of what may be accomplished by forestry, an example which we may hope in time to imitate, and a guide to direct our efforts. But we can not expect for a considerable length of time to accomplish the results obtained in Europe, and such systems of forestry as will accomplish them we can hope to form only in the course of natural development, and not by a sudden revolution of our present methods. There is no doubt that the best forests are produced by systems of management similar to those practiced abroad; but in most cases the expense involved in their establishment is so great that we must at first use rougher methods and be satisfied with imperfect results.

DEFINITION OF FORESTRY.

In order to correct the impression that European methods are absolutely necessary for the proper management of the forests in this country, a number of enthusiasts have gone so far as to define ordinary lumbering as forestry. This is fully as faulty as to say that there can be no forestry without using European methods. In its real significance, forestry conveys the idea of the continual use of the land for the purpose of producing forests. Thus, when a farmer thins his wood lot intelligently with the idea of sparing the small, thrifty timber he is practicing forestry. His method of work may not be the best but it is nevertheless forestry, just as crude farming is agriculture. When the farmer strips his stump land and holds it for successive crops of cord wood or hoop poles, or when a lumberman restricts the cutting of timber under a certain size in order to utilize the growth of the small trees, each is practicing forestry. But when a landowner cuts down a forest with no intention of utilizing the land for future crops of timber, it is no more forestry than it is agriculture when a farmer cuts the grass in a mountain meadow one year and then abandons it.

The efforts of the American forester should be directed not toward the immediate introduction of European methods, but to devising systems

FIG. 1.—GOOD AND BAD CUTTING. WHITNEY PRESERVE.

The small Spruce on the right has been left to seed up the opening made by the removal of the larger trees, but the stumps have been cut much higher than was necessary.

FIG. 2.—A GROUP OF YOUNG SPRUCE LEFT AFTER LUMBERING. WHITNEY PRESERVE.

of management which can be adopted by landowners at once, and which are capable of development as the conditions of the market allow. In other words, what is needed is an American system of forestry. It has been named an American system, because it must be adapted to American conditions, and in many cases it will differ radically from any practiced in Europe. Rules which are considered axiomatic abroad must often be set aside, and frequently results which could be obtained by the expenditure of a small amount of money must be sacrificed because the owner of the forest can not afford to make the investment. A sustained yield, an allotment of the forest into divisions, a permanent road system, the accessibility of all parts of the forest at one time, fire lines, improvement cuttings, and the like, which are usually considered a necessary part of forest management, each must, in many instances, be given up as impracticable for the present.

PRACTICAL FORESTRY IN THE ADIRONDACKS.

Just what can be accomplished in the way of forest management depends primarily on the ownership of the land. In the Adirondacks the land is owned by the State of New York, lumber companies, private individuals, and clubs. The position of the various classes of forest owners in regard to practical forestry is considered in the pages following, with special reference to the two tracts which form the subject of this report.

POSITION OF THE STATE OF NEW YORK REGARDING THE PRACTICE OF FORESTRY.

The chief purpose of the State of New York in maintaining large preserves is to protect the important watersheds and to provide a future supply of timber. The revenue which could be derived from the sale of lumber is a secondary consideration. The State can go further than the private individual in the direction of systematic forestry, for it can afford to make investments with the expectation of but small profits, or it can wait many years before realizing anything at all. Moreover, it may be satisfied with indirect returns in the general benefit to the community. The New York State holdings in the Adirondacks now exceed 1,100,000 acres, and are being increased as fast as appropriations can be obtained for the purpose. At present the constitution of New York prohibits the cutting of timber on State land, so that its management consists only in protecting the forest from fire and theft. But undoubtedly the constitution will in time be changed so as to permit conservative lumbering on the State preserve. Were this possible, the system of management which would be practical at the present time would necessarily be very simple, and would not differ to any great degree from that which can now be used by lumbermen and other private owners. The general plan for cutting Spruce should be the same as that presented in the working plan given in this report, namely, to remove the old timber above a certain diameter, and, where necessary, to leave selected trees above this size for seed. In the present working plan 10 inches at 3 feet from the ground has been made the average minimum limit for cutting. The State of New York, however, could afford to leave standing all trees under 12, or if necessary all under 14 inches in diameter; in other words, could leave a larger amount of money invested in the forest than the private owner.

The State of New York could, further, carry on thinnings for the improvement of the trees left standing, rather than for a profit from the sale of the timber. Thus the removal of many one-log Spruce trees 6 to 10 inches in diameter, which are usually left standing by the lumbermen, would benefit the forest to a considerable extent by giving more growing space and light to the trees which remain. In the same way small trees which could be used for pulp often stand in dense thickets, and a thinning of one-fifth or more of the crop would enable the remainder to grow much more rapidly. If a contractor were obliged to cut these trees he would undoubtedly raise his contract price. The State of New York could pay this price for the benefit of the forest, but at present most private individuals could not afford to make such an investment. Under certain circumstances the State could girdle some of the large crooked hardwoods which are crowding small Spruces and Pines, or if necessary cut them down; but for a lumberman in the Adirondacks such work would not be profitable under the present conditions.

The State would have a special advantage over the private owner in being able to enforce stricter regulations on the contractors in regard to the careful construction of roads, sparing the small growth in felling timber, in building skidways, bridges, etc., and lopping the branches from the tops as a protection against fire. The lumberman can carry out these regulations only so far as they do not to any great extent affect the cost of logging. Moreover, the State could employ a much larger force of experts to superintend the marking of timber and to watch the work of the contractors, or, in other words, could take better care of the forest than the private individual.

The time will undoubtedly come when the State of New York will carry on extensive operations in restocking denuded areas by sowing and planting. It is stated on page 19 that forest planting by most private owners in the Adirondacks would not, in the judgment of the writer, be wise business policy. Whether it would be profitable for the State of New York to restock denuded areas artificially is a question which will be definitely settled by the experiments now being carried on in the Adirondacks under the direction of Cornell University.

POSITION OF THE PRIVATE OWNER REGARDING THE PRACTICE OF FORESTRY.

The only reason for lumbermen and most private owners to adopt forestry is the financial one. Private individuals and clubs, to whom the income from the forest is less important than its preservation, are in the same position as the State. But lumbermen have invested their money in forest land or stumpage as a business matter, and unless the ultimate returns are greater from forest management than from the ordinary methods of lumbering they can not be expected to consider it at all. Where forest fires burn over the land repeatedly, as in many localities in the United States, no business man can be expected to leave the small trees, which can be sold even at a small profit, to grow to large timber and to distribute seed. In the same way lumbermen will not cut their land with the idea of reaping a second crop of timber in places where the taxes are so high as to more than counterbalance the amount gained through careful lumbering.

In certain sections lumber and paper companies have invested large sums of money in mill plants, and the continuance of their business depends on the future supply of timber. Such companies would find it most profitable to lumber their land in such a way that they could cut successive crops of wood every 20 to 30 years; in other words, to manage their lands along the lines of forestry. In the same way it would be folly for a lumberman to strip his land and practically ruin its sale value, if, by leaving the small trees, he could sell it to the State, paper companies, or sportsmen for a high price.

Hitherto many lumbermen who have looked up the matter of forestry have not adopted it because they have been unable to make a compromise with the foresters. Either they have wished to entirely strip the land of timber or the foresters have insisted upon certain measures which the lumbermen could not afford. Every plan of forest management in this country must be in a measure a compromise between the owner of the forest and the forester. The former must consent to leave a certain amount of capital invested in the forest in the form of growing wood, obtaining his returns from the sale of merchantable timber after the necessary period of growth has passed, or from the increased value of the land. The forester in his turn must give up certain operations which would benefit the forest.

OBJECTS OF FOREST MANAGEMENT.

For the two tracts of forest land considered in this report a plan of management was required that would satisfy three parties, namely, the owners, the contractors, and the forester.

THE OWNERS' OBJECT.

The object of the owners, in the case in hand, is to cut as much timber as possible without injuring the productive power of the forest. The land has been heavily taxed and has yielded no return. If the larger timber is removed the taxes will be reduced and there will be a substantial money return from the forest. The object is to convert the unproductive portion of the capital, the old timber, into ready money, to be invested elsewhere, and to leave the productive part of the forest, the young timber, in a condition to accumulate interest in the form of added wood. The owners are willing to do without the profits which would accrue from the sale of the small trees in order that the productive capacity of the forest may remain unimpaired. The money which is thus left invested in the forest the owners expect to recover with interest through the increased value of the land.

THE CONTRACTOR'S OBJECT.

In the cases under consideration the lumbering is done under contract, and the contractor carries on the work himself or sublets it to jobbers. Inasmuch as the contractor or jobber obtains a certain sum per standard for the logs, it is obvious that he receives the greatest profit from the large trees, because the cost per standard of cutting, skidding, and hauling is less for the large than the small logs. There is no profit at all for the contractor in cutting small one-log trees and but little in small two-log trees. He is perfectly willing, therefore, to accept a contract to cut only the large trees.

THE FORESTER'S OBJECT.

The object of the forester is to obtain for the owner a large revenue from the timber, but at the same time to leave the forest in a condition to produce a second crop in a comparatively short time, and to reseed the openings made in lumbering with young growth of valuable species.

MEASURES WHICH CAN NOT BE CARRIED OUT IN NEHASANE PARK AND THE WHITNEY PRESERVE.

In order to accomplish the object of the owners on the two tracts under consideration, and to secure favorable contracts for cutting the timber, a number of measures, usually considered a necessary part of forest management, must be given up. These are:

The maintenance of a sustained annual yield.

The removal of dead and unsound trees.

Thinnings and improvement cuttings.

Permanent roads.

Planting.

Fire lines.

That these measures are not practicable on the two tracts will be shown in the discussion following.

THE MAINTENANCE OF A SUSTAINED ANNUAL YIELD.

One of the first principles of forestry is to cut timber in such a way that the productive capacity of the forest is not impaired. The majority of advocates of forestry have interpreted this principle as meaning that an equal return should be obtained from the forest every year. As a matter of fact, the object of forestry is attained if the land is kept stocked with trees and is producing valuable material to its utmost capacity, whether an equal return is obtained every year or not.

In Europe a constant, approximately equal, annual income from the forest is deemed of first importance, especially on large tracts. There is always in such places a steady market which has to be supplied with timber. Moreover, a large force of expert foresters and woodsmen is employed to care for the forest, and it is extremely desirable that they find steady employment. It is desirable also that there be an annual income to cover the taxes and interest on the invested capital.

In order to secure this income the merchantable timber, which could be taken out without injuring the forest, is not removed in one year, but the cuttings are distributed so that an approximately equal amount is cut annually. Thus, if a tract of 100,000 acres were stocked with Pine, ripe at 100 years of age, an amount equivalent to the yield of 1,000 acres would be cut each year.

The forests in which this provision is most strenuously observed are owned by the Government, but it frequently happens that a private owner, requiring a large sum of money or a certain quantity of wood at once, cuts so heavily into the forest capital that no further income can be realized for a considerable length of time. By so doing he does not necessarily injure the productive power of the forest, but instead of spreading his cuttings over a large number of years, cuts the whole or a considerable portion of the area at one time.

In this country the forests owned by States or the Federal Government should, in very many cases, be managed so as to yield a constant annual return just as in Europe; and the same applies to many large lumber or paper companies which own extensive tracts of land and which require a certain amount of timber every year to supply their mills. But for most private owners the only practical system of management is one in which the returns are obtained periodically.

The two preserves considered in this report are covered with virgin forest, in which much of the timber is very old and on the decline. Here, as in any original forest, the growth of the trees is just about equalized by the loss through decay and wind or other destructive natural agencies. The forest is therefore virtually at a standstill, or, in other words, is accumulated capital which is producing no interest. If the old trees are cut and utilized before they decay and are replaced by young, thrifty, growing specimens, the forest becomes at once productive capital. It is obvious that it should be placed on this basis as quickly as possible, or, in other words, that the old timber should be removed as rapidly as it can be marketed. To illustrate the proposition more concretely, the growth obtained under a system of annual sustained yield may be compared with that under the method of intermittent sustained yield. If the timber on the tracts discussed in this report were cut to 10 inches in diameter, it has been calculated that the same returns could be obtained again in 36 years.[1] If the principle of a sustained annual yield were carried out it would be necessary to cut about one thirty-sixth of the total crop each year. There would be at the end of that period 36 years' increment on one thirty-sixth of the tract, 35 years' increment on one thirty-sixth, 34 years' increment on one thirty-sixth, etc., or, to strike a general average, 18 years' growth on the whole tract. If the whole area were cut in one year there would be 36 years' growth on the entire tract at the end of 36 years. If the annual growth were 0.5 standards per acre on, say, 5,000 acres, 36 years' growth would amount to 90,000 standards, as against 45,000 standards under the system of a sustained annual yield. In this example the principle that in virgin forest the growth is equalized by the loss through decay and destructive natural agencies, which is entirely true over a large tract, is applied to small areas. In individual sections it is probable that on account of windfall the loss will very much exceed the growth. There will be other instances, however, where the trees are mostly young and thrifty, and the growth will so far exceed the decay as to counterbalance the loss elsewhere. (Pl. III).

A further consideration in favor of cutting over the whole area in a short time is the question of taxes. In the Adirondacks they are reduced about one-half after lumbering. By the same reasoning as in the foregoing discussion, under the system of a sustained annual yield, full taxes would have been paid on one-half the area at the end of 36 years. Under the other system the taxes would be lowered on the whole tract at the end of the first year. Moreover, the cost of logging would be much less if the timber were taken out in one or a few years and much better contract prices could be made. The cost of superintendence, marking, etc., would likewise be proportionately smaller under the intermittent system.

REMOVAL OF DEAD AND UNSOUND TREES.

The class of thinnings known as cleanings, by which the dead, dying, and unsound trees are removed, is considered very important in Europe. Often the entire tract is cleaned every year or within short periods. The purpose is twofold: First, to utilize the wood before it decays, and second, to prevent the breeding of insects. Inasmuch as the dead trees can not be utilized in the present instance, their removal would be very expensive and the object attained would not justify the outlay. The cutting of unsound timber is also impracticable, because such trees in most places can not be utilized. If left standing, on the other hand, they help to shade the ground and distribute a certain amount of seed.

THINNINGS AND IMPROVEMENT CUTTINGS.

It frequently happens in the Adirondacks that young Spruces of even age grow in very dense masses, and if some of the trees were

---

[1] See page 37.

THRIFTY YOUNG SPRUCE AND PINE COMING UP AFTER A WINDFALL. NEHASANE PARK.

removed the remainder would grow much more rapidly. If these could be sold they should be cut, but otherwise they should be left standing, for the advantage resulting from their removal would not justify cutting them at a loss or without profit. Such cuttings are technically known as thinnings.

There are, further, in the forest many young Spruces which have grown under hardwood trees and which need light and room for their proper development. The girdling or felling of the hardwoods, which are unsound, crooked, and will never be of any value whatever, and which are killing young Spruce and Pine, has been advocated by a number of men. It is certain that their presence means the death of a large number of young trees which might develop into valuable timber; but in most cases the private owner can not afford to cut them unless the material can be sold. Where this class of timber is not marketable, as nearly everywhere in the Adirondacks, the cutting or girdling would involve a considerable expenditure of money from which no immediate returns could be obtained. If the trees were girdled, it is estimated that they would cost at least 1 cent each. In many instances where the branches actually interfere with the small trees girdling would not be sufficient, in which case felling would be necessary. It would be desirable also to trim them in order to prevent danger from fire, all of which would cost from 2 to 5 cents per tree. In most cases the felling of hardwoods would destroy a considerable amount of young growth, and frequently it would be impossible to fell them without injuring the very trees which it is desired to favor.

This question of girdling and cutting undesirable hardwoods was studied with extreme care, and it was estimated that the work could not be done properly under 25 cents per acre. On a tract of 100,000 acres this means the expenditure of $25,000. The writer is convinced that for the two tracts under consideration such an investment would not pay. The removal of the less desirable trees, as described above, for the purpose of improving the condition of the trees which remain is called an improvement cutting.

PERMANENT ROADS.

In Europe it has long been the policy to adopt a system of permanent roads; in fact, this is considered one of the most important measures in a well regulated forest. It will be many years, however, before such roads can be built in the lumber woods in the Adirondacks, for it would not pay to maintain them unless they are needed constantly; and in most cases lumber operations can be carried on in a particular section only at long intervals.

PLANTING.

The lumbermen have frequently been impressed with the idea that planting forms an essential part of forestry. In some parts of Europe the forests are regenerated almost entirely by artificial means, and natural reproduction is nearly always supplemented by planting or sowing. The results of planting are without doubt most satisfactory, but for lumbermen in the Adirondacks it can not be considered on account of the great outlay it involves.

FIRE LINES.

The forests in Europe are usually cut up into divisions which range in size from 25 to over 100 acres, and are separated by roads or lines. The purpose of this division is to facilitate the description of the forest and the location of cuttings, to make the whole forest readily accessible, and to aid in putting out fires. The opening of similar strips has been advocated in a number of instances for regions in this country where the danger from fire is great. If well kept up, they would be a great help in putting out fires, but in the Adirondacks the expense of their construction and maintenance would make them impracticable for most private owners. It may be said in this connection that in certain sections, especially in the Southern States, the burning of fire strips is entirely practicable and advisable.

THE SYSTEM OF MANAGEMENT ADVOCATED FOR THE TWO TRACTS.

The provisions of European forestry, just enumerated as impracticable at present in the Adirondacks, have hitherto been the chief barriers in the way of the adoption of forestry by lumbermen. When the forester sees that in many cases they must be given up, a system satisfactory to all can be devised. In the present case the owners of Nehasane Park and the Whitney Preserve will be satisfied with the income from the timber above 10 inches in diameter, and on this basis they can obtain satisfactory contracts for cutting the timber. The forester is satisfied from a careful study that the Spruce over 10 inches in diameter can be cut without injuring the forest, provided certain trees over this size are left for seed. Although successive crops could be obtained from the land at shorter intervals if 12 instead of 10 inches were made the average minimum limit of cutting, the owners prefer to wait a longer time for the second crop and to get a larger return at once. The system of cutting recommended for the two tracts is, briefly, to remove the Spruce measuring 10 inches and over in diameter at 3 feet from the ground, except certain trees which are needed to seed up the openings made in lumbering.

PURPOSE OF A WORKING PLAN.

The object of forestry is to remove the timber from a given tract in such a way that repeated crops can be obtained for an indefinite period without decreasing the producing power of the forest. In order to do this it is necessary to know just what trees must be left standing to form a basis for future growth and to seed the ground to valuable species. It is necessary to know what the rate of growth of the trees left in the forest will be after the first cutting in order to determine how soon the second crop can be obtained, and also to know what new growth will come in to take the place of the trees which have been removed. The purpose of making a working plan is to study questions of the growth, reproduction, and general character of the important trees, and to devise a system of cutting which will enable the owner to make a profit from the land and at the same time to secure the permanence of the forest.

DESCRIPTION OF THE TRACTS UNDER CONSIDERATION.

Two tracts are included in the working plan presented in this report, namely, Nehasane Park in Hamilton and Herkimer counties, N. Y., belonging to Dr. W. Seward Webb, and the preserve belonging to Hon. William C. Whitney in Hamilton County.

NEHASANE PARK.

This is a body of forest land, roughly triangular in outline, with the longest side to the north (Pl. IV). It lies in the west central portion of the Adirondack Mountains of northern New York, and is traversed in a northeasterly direction by the New York Central and Hudson River Railroad (Adirondack and St. Lawrence Division). About two-thirds of the area is in townships 37 and 38 of Hamilton County, while the western third lies in Herkimer County, townships 42 and 43. From east to west the park stretches from Little Tupper Lake to Big Rock Lake and includes the latter, together with Lake Lila, Lake Nehasane (Pl. VI, fig. 2), and a portion of the head waters of Beaver River. Other waters of the park drain through Little Tupper Lake to the Raquette River and through Cranberry Lake to the east branch of the Oswegatchie. Both these lakes are outside its boundaries. The general elevation is from 1,700 to 2,000 feet above sea level.

The whole park includes an area of about 40,000 acres. The general character of the country is hilly and somewhat broken, with low swampy tracts near the streams and lakes. Numerous knolls and ridges, from a few yards to over 300 feet in height, rise from the lower ground. In general the ridges or series of ridges run northeast and southwest. Low rounded knolls rising above swampy ground are very frequent. More level areas, or flats, are of considerable extent; some of them low and rolling and covered with glacial bowlders. There are numbers of broad flat ridges. The higher hills are for the most part conical, with small tops, or consist of long narrow ridges. The southerly slopes are apt to be rocky, abrupt, or often even precipitous. The northerly slopes are more gradual. This country shows in many ways the effect of the ice with which it was once covered. The soil is a glacial drift, and the manner in which the rocks have been smoothed off and the rounded bowlders deposited on the flats and on the south slopes affords similar evidence. The shape of the ridges is due to glaciation.

Granite, varying much in color and texture, is the principal rock. The typical soil of the park is glacial gravel or sand, replaced by loam in richer situations. On steep slopes it is thin, and what there is usually collects in hollows, on benches, on the uphill side of rocks and trees, or in rocky crevices. On moderate slopes and high flats the soil is deep, fresh, and porous; on low flats, moist and often deep; on less level flats, thin on account of the bowlders, and in swamps a deep muck.

The conditions of heat, moisture, and ventilation are such in the dense and damp Adirondack forest that the waste materials which drop from the trees and other forest vegetation decay slowly after falling. The result is a mass of partially disintegrated vegetable matter which has been accumulating for years, and which may cover the ground to a depth of several feet. This layer, deeper on low than on high ground, often becomes acid humus in the swamps.

THE WHITNEY PRESERVE.

This tract of approximately 68,000 acres is included within what is known as the Totten and Crossfield purchase, town of Long Lake, Hamilton County, N. Y. It comprises township 36, the northwest quarter of township 35, the greater part of township 23, a portion of the triangle east of township 23, and a few lots in township 21 (Pl. V).

The greater part of the preserve slopes toward Little Tupper Lake, but a considerable portion sheds its water into Long Lake, Forked Lake, and the Raquette River.

The tract is characterized by a large number of lakes and small ponds. The largest of these is Little Tupper Lake (Pl. VI, fig. 1), which is about 6 miles long and about 1 mile wide, into which the water drains from the northern portion of the preserve. Little Tupper Lake empties into Round Pond, and this in turn into Big Tupper Lake. The water eventually reaches the Raquette River. The southern part of the preserve sheds its water also into the Raquette River, chiefly through Forked and Long lakes. Salmon Lake empties into Beaver River through Little Salmon and Lila lakes. In general the land is a high rolling plateau, broken by a few high mountains and a number of long, rather low, broad ridges, which are interspersed with numerous ponds and swamps. On townships 36 and 23, with the exception of Salmon Mountain, Buck Mountain, and a few insignificant ridges, almost the entire area is of this rolling character. About Forked Lake the topography is more rugged and the ridges and hills higher.

The prevailing rock is gneiss, which accounts in part for the comparatively gentle topography.

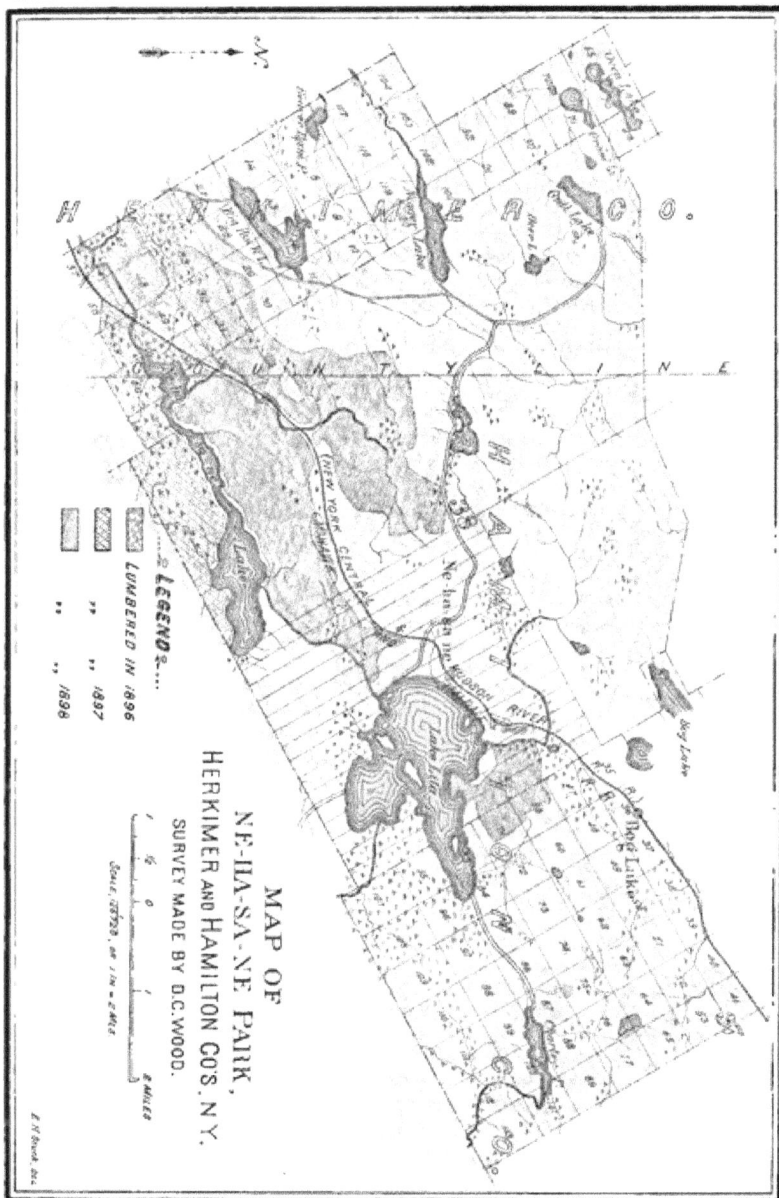

MAP OF
NE-HA-SA-NE PARK,
HERKIMER AND HAMILTON CO'S. N.Y.
SURVEY MADE BY D.C. WOOD.

LEGEND

LUMBERED IN 1896
" " 1897
" " 1898

Scale, 63360, or 1 in = 1 mile

8 MILES

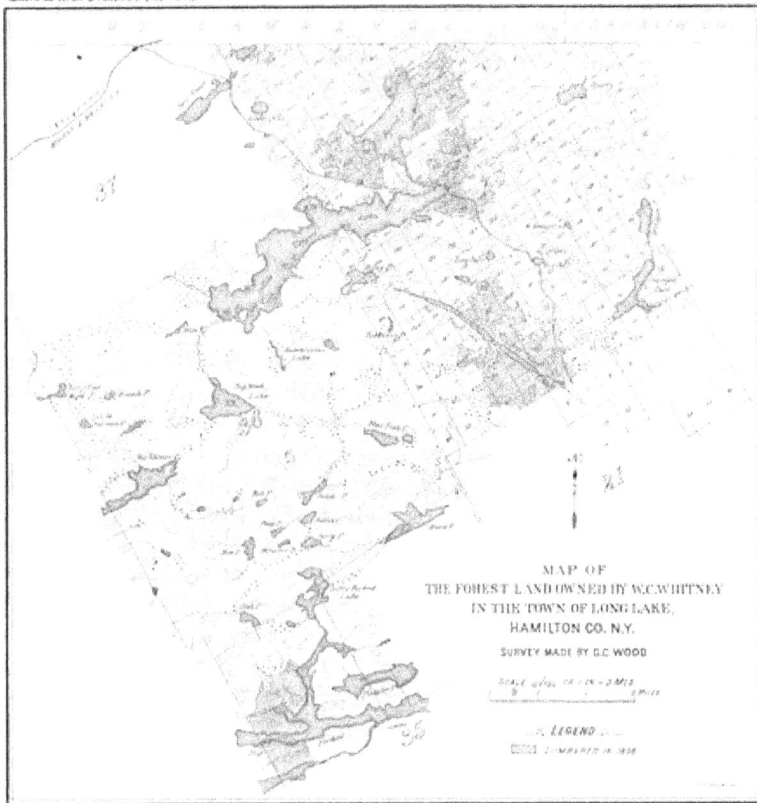

MAP OF
THE FOREST LAND OWNED BY W.C.WHITNEY
IN THE TOWN OF LONG LAKE,
HAMILTON CO. N.Y.

SURVEY MADE BY G.C WOOD

LEGEND

DESCRIPTION OF THE FOREST.

FACTORS CONTROLLING THE DISTRIBUTION OF SPECIES.

The occurrence of the various species within the range of their general distribution is primarily determined by the local climate, the situation and soil, and the qualities inherent in each species to carry on the struggle for existence. Often, however, where the conditions are otherwise equally favorable, it depends on purely accidental circumstances. Within the range of the distribution of each tree there is a region where the influences which control vegetable life are especially favorable to it, and here, as a result, the best development is found as regards yield, quality of wood, reproductive capacity, tolerance of shade, ability to grow in poor soils, and all other sylvicultural characteristics.

The species whose regions of best development include the Adirondacks are Spruce,[1] Hard Maple, Beech, and Yellow Birch. Other species, though not necessarily inferior to these trees in their sylvicultural qualities, do not reach as high a development as in some other sections where the climate and other influences are more favorable to their growth. Those just enumerated usually win in the struggle for the occupancy of the situation suited to their requirements, and there form the principal part of the forest. This contest for the possession of the ground is most determined on the better classes of soil, because there a greater number of species find the possibilities for their development, and are more tolerant of shade and bear seed more abundantly than on poor soils. Where other things are equal, the trees which can bear the most shade usually win in the contest. Thus on the better soils Hard Maple and Beech have the advantage over Yellow Birch because the latter is less tolerant of shade. They also have the advantage over Spruce, partly on account of their greater tolerance, but also because the conditions of reproduction in the hardwood forest are not favorable to the latter. Spruce and Birch therefore occupy a relatively small proportion of the forest on the best soils. The following list gives the relative degree of tolerance of the important trees in this section of the Adirondacks, beginning with those which require the most light: Tamarack, Poplar, Bird Cherry, Ash, Black Cherry, White Pine, Birch, Soft Maple, Balsam, Spruce, Hemlock, Beech, Hard Maple.

Next to tolerance of shade the ability to grow on inferior soil is the most important of the qualities which enable a tree to carry on the struggle for existence. Yellow Birch is usually crowded out on the best soils by Beech and Hard Maple, but it is able to thrive in places where the latter are unable to grow. In the same way Spruce is crowded out in many places by hardwoods, but it maintains its position in the forest by occupying the less favorable situations and soils, where fewer species are able to exist and the contest for the possession of the ground is less intense. The predominance of certain trees on

[1] The generic word Spruce, used throughout the report, refers to Red Spruce, *Picea rubra* (Poir) Diet.

inferior soil has led to an impression that they prefer such to rich
ground. The fact is that they are not found in other situations because
they are prevented from growing there by the more tolerant species,
or because the soil does not contain the degree of moisture necessary
to their existence. The relative demands of the most important species
on the quality of soil are shown in the following list, which begins
with the most exacting: Black Cherry, Hard Maple, Beech, Soft
Maple, Birch, White Pine, Balsam, Hemlock, Spruce.

Many kinds of trees are able to hold their position in the forest by
their great reproductive power, as, for example, the Poplar. This tree
has an extremely light seed, which is blown for great distances by the
wind. It is thus able to seize upon openings made by fire or otherwise,
and, inasmuch as it thrives on extremely barren soil, it usually forms
an important part in the first forest growth on burned land after a fire.

The rapid growth in height is an important factor in enabling some
trees to hold their own against other species. Thus, Pine and Tamarack, both intolerant trees in the Adirondacks, are able to grow above
the more tolerant kinds, if they can obtain a footing at all, and in this way
their crowns have the degree of light necessary for their development.

It frequently happens, however, that the composition of the forest
in a particular place is not determined so much by the influences discussed above as by accidental circumstances. If, for example, an
opening has been made by the wind, the kind of trees which will come
up depends in a large measure on the seed which happens to be in
the ground and on what species happen to be in the neighborhood.
Other circumstances, as the fact that it is a favorable seed year for
certain trees, the direction of the wind, etc., may be the controlling
influences. It is through such chances as these that intolerant trees
are able to obtain a footing in mixture with tolerant kinds, and scattered individuals, whose regions of best development are elsewhere,
become a part of the forest.

FOREST TYPES.

If nature is left undisturbed, the same type of forest will tend to be
produced on the same classes of situation and soil in a specified region.
There will be variations within the type, but the characteristic features
of the forest will remain constant—that is, the predominant species,
density, habit of trees, reproduction, character of undergrowth, etc.
So characteristic and distinct are these forest types that an expert can
describe the general character of the forest if he knows the region, the
altitude, the soil, and the situation; and, vice versa, can describe the
character of the soil, situation, etc., if he knows the type of forest. If
a portion of the forest is destroyed by fire, wind, or otherwise, the type
may for the time being be changed; but if left undisturbed it will
revert to its original form, provided the condition of the soil is not per-
manently changed. Thus, in the Adirondacks, a group of Spruce and
Pine on an island may be replaced after a fire by White Birch and

FIG. 1.—WHITE PINE ON SMALL ISLANDS IN LITTLE TUPPER LAKE. WHITNEY PRESERVE.

FIG. 2.—A GENERAL VIEW OF LAKE NEHASANE.

Poplar. After a time, however, the former will creep back and grow under the thin cover of the Birch and Poplar, and eventually crowd them out. A good illustration of the same principle is found in Massachusetts, where in many sections the White Pine formed an important feature in the original forest. After the Pine was cut off the hardwoods predominated in the second growth. Now, however, there is abundant evidence that the White Pine is increasing in quantity, and if the woods were left untouched the original type would return.

It is possible to differentiate the forest in the Adirondacks into a considerable number of types, but for simplicity only four have been recognized. These are as follows: Swamp land, Spruce flats, Hardwood land, and Spruce slopes. The names chosen for these types describe rather the situation on which they are found than the forest itself. Lumbermen are, however, accustomed to speak of swamps, hardwood ridges, etc., and these familiar terms have been kept as far as possible.

SWAMP LAND.

All low flats with wet, spongy soils are comprised under this head. The characteristic species are Red Spruce, Black Spruce, Balsam, and Tamarack, some Soft Maple and Pine, and scattered Black Ash and Cedar. There are numerous small elevated flats and knolls within the limits of the swamps which really should be classified as Spruce flats, but which are too small to be segregated in making estimates. On these are found Red Spruce, Hemlock, Birch, and sometimes Beech and Hard Maple.

The Red Spruce is usually rather short on swamp lands, partly on account of the character of the soil, but also because it is comparatively young. Spruce grows slowly in swamps, but the principal reason why only a few large trees are found is because they are blown down before they reach maturity. Occasionally, however, patches of old Spruce are found which have succeeded in withstanding the winds. These trees are fairly tall and clear of branches, but generally of comparatively small diameter. For Spruce over 10 inches the average diameter is about 13 inches and the average height under 60 feet.

Balsam, like the swamp Spruce, is, as a rule, relatively young, and in consequence small. It is a short-lived tree in the Adirondacks, and the larger specimens are frequently unsound. It grows usually in dense stands, often nearly pure. The average diameter for trees over 10 inches in diameter is about 11.5 inches.

Black Spruce is, in the Adirondacks, a small spindling tree, never reaching a merchantable size. It is found growing almost pure in low wet marshes, and is seldom found mixed with other species.

Throughout the swamps may be found remnants of an old forest of Tamarack, either as dead standing stubs or as decaying logs on the ground. Some years ago the greater part of the old timber was killed by a sawfly worm, which defoliated the trees, and now it is almost impossible to find a live specimen over 10 inches in diameter. Here and there may be found clumps or scattered specimens of young Tamarack, but even these trees have in many cases been attacked by insects and are dying down from the top. (Pl. VII. fig. 2.) The Tamarack is followed, on the less saturated ground, by Spruce, Balsam, and sometimes White Pine. Along the low inlets the second growth is usually young Tamarack and Soft Maple.

Black Ash is very exacting regarding soil. It is almost never found growing naturally, except on wet soil. The trees in the portion of the Adirondacks included in this working plan are of moderate size, on an average about 13 inches in diameter, and are frequently unsound.

Cedar is not an important element in the forest and is very much localized in its distribution. It is found about a number of the lakes which are surrounded by low banks. Thus, on the east side of Lake Lila, in Nehasane Park, and on Bottle, Flatfish, Stony, and some other ponds in the Whitney Preserve there is a fringe of White Cedar. The trees are usually rather short and scrubby and have a very quick taper. Their average diameter is about 14.5 inches for trees over 10 inches though. The few Birch which succeed in growing on low ground are crooked and unsound. The other species found within the limits of swamp land occur chiefly on slight elevations, and are discussed under Spruce flats.

The following table, which gives the measurements of a sample plot made by the writer in 1896 at Santa Clara, N. Y., is an excellent illustration of a typical swamp in the Adirondacks. The table also shows the average rate of growth of swamp Spruce of different diameters.

Acre measurements (1 acre) on cut-over swamp lands at Santa Clara, N. Y.

[From "The Adirondack Spruce."]

(This land was cut over in 1891, at which time two Spruce trees with an estimated yield of 1.6 standards were removed. Situation: Spruce swamp. Soil: Wet. Balsam bunched on one side of the acre. No trees show increased growth after cutting.)

Diameter.	Material cut in 1896.				Mean annual growth in diameter last 10 years.	Material left after cutting (number of trees).			
	Spruce trees.	Average height.	Cubic feet.	Standards.		Spruce.	Balsam.	Cedar.	Birch.
Inches.		Feet.			Inches.				
1									
2						66	187	1	
3						78	140	3	
4						46	98	5	
5	2	33.7	4.9	0.06	0.12	28	38	6	
6	30	37.8	129.1	1.95	.08	9	15		
7	41	37.8	230.6	4.58	.104		7	8	1
8	35	41.7	269.8	5.37	.11	1	3	2	1
9	26	43.6	272.5	5.92	.10		4		3
10	18	48.3	243.8	5.17	.116	1	2		
11	5	51.3	98.2	2.10	.132			1	
12	3	49.7	115.5	2.29	.132				
13	1	50.4	22.2	.45	.13				
14	1	54.9	27.7	.55	.08				
15	2	49.6	57.8	1.24	.16				
16	0								
17	1	45.7	41.6	.86	.04				
Total..	167		1,364.7	30.54		229	495	26	7

FIG. 1.—WHITE PINE GROWING ON ONE OF THE POINTS OF FORKED LAKE. WHITNEY PRESERVE.

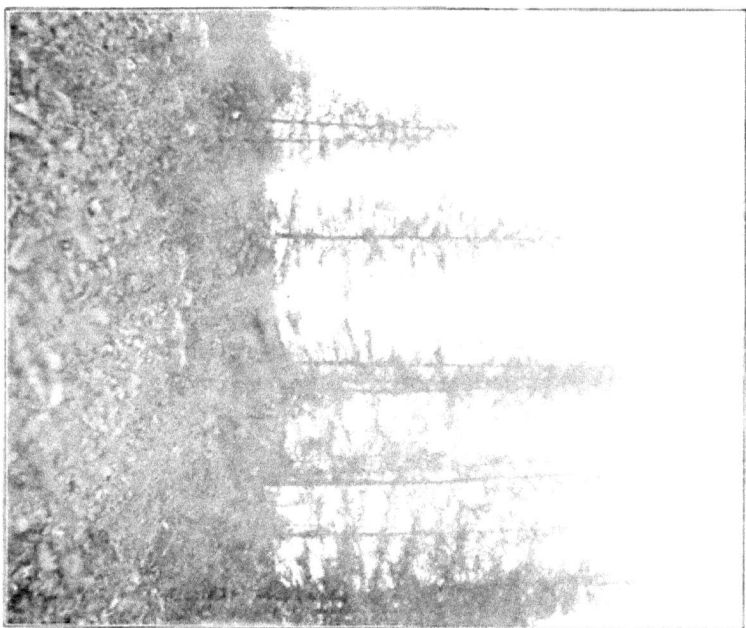

FIG. 2.—YOUNG TAMARACK DYING DOWN FROM TOP FROM THE ATTACKS OF A SAWFLY WORM. WHITNEY PRESERVE.

The following table gives the result of 225 acre measurements made on swamp land in Nehasane Park, in 1897, during the investigation of the Adirondack Spruce mentioned on page 10. The acres were measured off in the form of strips, so that many slight elevations were included, which accounts for the presence in the table of Hard Maple and Beech:

Acre measurements (average of 225 acres) on swamp lands.

[From "The Adirondack Spruce."]

(Average number of trees per acre, percentage in mixture, and average and maximum diameters of all sound trees 10 inches and over in diameter breast high.)

Name of species.	Average number of trees per acre.	Percentage of each species.	Average diameter breast high.	Maximum diameter breast high.
			Inches.	Inches.
Spruce	34.00	47.94	12.8	27
Birch	13.00	18.33	15.4	36
Beech	2.40	3.38	12.8	25
Hard Maple	2.40	3.38	13.2	29
Hemlock	5.10	7.19	16.5	35
Balsam	9.49	13.25	11.4	24
Soft Maple	3.00	4.23	13.1	30
White Pine	.36	.51	17.1	37
Ash	.64	.90	13.4	23
Cedar	.60	.85	14.5	28
Cherry	.03	.04	19.4	33
Average of all species	70.93	100.00	14.5	29.5
Average of all species except Spruce	36.93	52.06	14.7	29.8

SPRUCE FLATS.

The level and rolling flats bordering on lakes, streams, and swamps have been designated as Spruce flats. As a rule, the soil is fresh and frequently moist. It is sometimes fairly deep, especially where it is chiefly composed of sand, but more often it is shallow and covered with stones and bowlders.

Spruce here reaches an intermediate development between that growing in swamps and on the higher ground. The trees are somewhat shorter than on the hardwood lands, and are more apt to be unsound.

The characteristic trees in mixture with Spruce are Birch, Soft Maple, White Pine, Hemlock, and some Balsam. Where Ash or a considerable amount of Balsam is found the forest approaches the swamp-land type, and where the Hard Maple occurs the land is usually elevated enough to be classed as hardwood land. Cedar, Cherry, and a few straggling Beech are not uncommon.

While there is a considerable amount of Birch on Spruce flats, it is rather short and scrubby, and is apt to be unsound. It is on Spruce flats that the most of the White Pine is found. It is usually said to grow in swamps, but most of the trees are on slight elevations, which are similar in the character of the forest to Spruce flats. Where the soil is sandy, as on the points projecting into lakes. Pine often forms the principal part of the forest growth. (Pl. VII. fig. 1.) An excellent illustration of this is found on Forked Lake, where the spurs of land which project into the lake are covered with an admirable growth of thrifty, but comparatively young. Pine. Another instance of the growth of Pine on Spruce flats is found on the small islands in the large lakes.

On the sandy shores of Little Tupper Lake there are a considerable number of Norway Pines. (Pl. VIII.) These trees are tall and clear boled, and reach an average diameter of about 15 to 18 inches. The distribution of this tree is very limited, and no specimens at all were seen in Nehasane Park.

Hemlock occurs most abundantly on Spruce flats, and it is here that the soundest specimens are found. It forms about 9 per cent of the total crop of trees over 10 inches in diameter. It is on Spruce flats also that Soft Maple reaches its best development.

The danger from windfall on Spruce flats is considerable, and young second growth is very common. It is in such circumstances that Spruce comes up almost pure. This is well illustrated in Nehasane Park, where, on the north side of the railroad, about 2 miles below Nehasane station, there is a considerable stretch of dense second-growth Spruce which has come up after a windfall. The reproduction of Spruce does not, however, always follow to this degree, for not far from the place just mentioned the second growth is composed almost exclusively of Birch and Soft Maple.

The following table gives the average measurements of 100 acres on Spruce flats, taken in 1897 in Nehasane Park:

Acre measurements (average of 100 acres) on Spruce flats.

[From "The Adirondack spruce."]

(Average number of trees per acre, percentage in mixture, and average and maximum diameters of all sound trees 10 inches and over in diameter breast high.)

Name of species.	Average number of trees per acre.	Percentage of each species.	Average diameter breast high.	Maximum diameter breast high.
			Inches.	Inches.
Spruce	29	45	13.5	27
Birch	12.70	19.71	16.4	34
Beech	5.60	8.69	13.4	22
Hard Maple	2.50	3.88	14	26
Hemlock	5.60	8.69	16.5	34
Balsam	5.80	9	11.3	18
Soft Maple	3	4.65	13.7	23
White Pine	.10	.15	21	45
Ash	.10	.15	13	16
Cherry	.05	.68	14.7	17
Average of all species	64.45	100	14.4	26.4
Average of all species except Spruce	35.45	55	14.6	26.3

PLATE VIII.

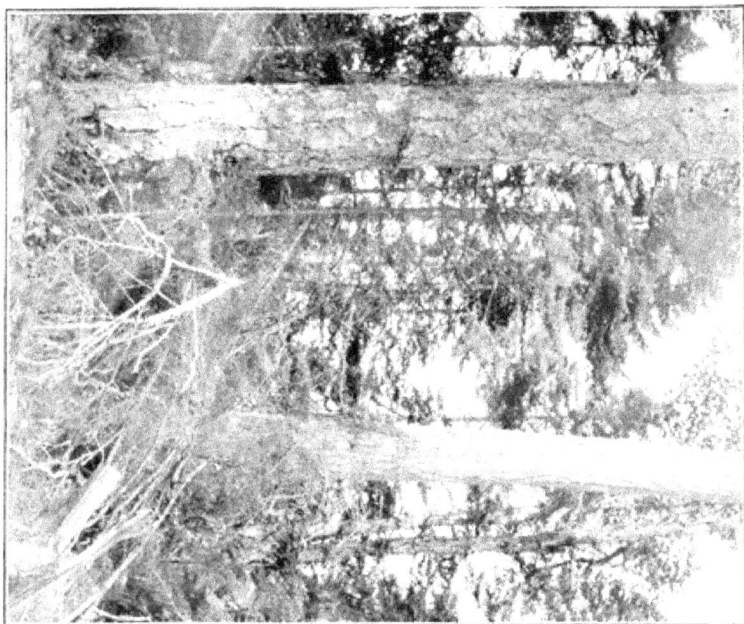

FIG. 1.— WHITE AND NORWAY PINE. WHITNEY PRESERVE.

FIG. 2.— NORWAY PINE, LITTLE TUPPER LAKE. WHITNEY PRESERVE.

HARDWOOD LAND.

On elevated benches and moderate slopes the forest is chiefly a deciduous growth mixed with a considerable quantity of Spruce and scattering Hemlock. (Pl. IX, fig. 1.) In such situations the richest soil is to be found, and here Spruce, though not the predominant species, reaches its greatest size. The largest Spruce seen on either tract was growing on a hardwood bench and measured 34 inches in diameter. The trees growing on the slopes are, as a rule, not as large as those on the high benches, but they usually have a greater clear length and a shorter crown.

The chief species on hardwood land besides the Spruce are Hard Maple, Beech, Birch, and scattered Hemlock, Soft Maple, and Cherry. (Pl. IX, fig. 2.)

In general the Spruce forms on the hardwood land in Nehasane Park about 30 per cent of the trees over 10 inches in diameter. The measurements from which this was taken included only those trees which were apparently sound. If the gnarled and unsound trees were included the proportion would be larger.

In the Whitney Preserve the hardwood forest contains a somewhat smaller proportion of Spruce than in Nehasane Park. The reason for this is that the land is less broken and irregular and there are a larger number of long, low ridges with moderate slopes on which the hardwoods thrive exceedingly well. On account of the great reproductive power and the tolerance of the hardwoods, they are able to occupy ground which is favorable to their growth often to the exclusion of other species. The insect pest, which occurred about 15 years ago, and of which mention is made on page 56, seems to have killed a large number of Spruce in the hardwood forest. The consequence is that in many places the Spruce has nearly all died out and the forest is composed almost exclusively of hardwoods. A number of sample acres were measured off in such places, and it was found that frequently there were no more than one or two Spruce trees per acre over 10 inches in diameter.

Wherever the land is considerably broken, as in Nehasane Park, there is generally a large proportion of Spruce and Yellow Birch, while Hard Maple and Beech are confined to the moderate northern slopes and bases of the ridges and to the high benches.

The following table gives the result of 442 acre measurements taken in Nehasane Park during the summer of 1897:

Acre measurements (average of 442 acres) on hardwood lands.

[From "The Adirondack Spruce."]

(Average number of trees per acre, percentage in mixture, and average and maximum diameters of all sound trees 10 inches and over in diameter breast high.)

Name of species.	Average number of trees per acre.	Percentage of each species.	Average diameter breast high.	Maximum diameter breast high.
			Inches.	Inches.
Spruce	29.00	36.84	13.1	32
Birch	15.00	19.06	17.8	42
Beech	16.40	20.84	13.7	30
Hard Maple	10.10	12.83	14.3	33
Hemlock	4.00	5.08	17.4	36
Balsam	1.70	2.16	11.4	21
Soft Maple	2.30	2.92	14.0	30
White Pine	.05	.06	13.6	33
Ash	.03	.04	12.4	24
Cherry	.13	.17	15.8	27
Average of all species	78.71	100.00	14.3	30.8
Average of all species except Spruce	49.71	63.16	14.3	30.7

SPRUCE SLOPES.

These comprise the steep slopes with thin, stony soil. It has elsewhere been pointed out that Beech and Hard Maple, the most persistent enemies of Spruce, have difficulty in growing on such soil. The forest in these situations is, therefore, chiefly composed of Spruce, with a few Yellow Birch in mixture, and with patches of Hemlock and Pine on the brows of the ridges. The Spruce is tall and clear, but usually of smaller diameter than on hardwood land. The largest specimens occur on the small benches and hollows, where the rich wash from the hillside has collected. On Spruce slopes the danger from windfall is very great, and in consequence the forest is frequently comparatively young, the old trees having been blown down.

The Birch which succeeds in maintaining a foothold on the steep Spruce slopes is of excellent quality. The trunks are long, clear, and sound.

The Hemlock and Pine are generally in patches on the brows of steep, abrupt slopes, and there is usually under them a smaller growth of Spruce. The Hemlock is of inferior quality to that on Spruce flats, on account of windshake, to which it is exposed in this situation.

In the following table, on the next page, which gives the average result of the measurements of 274 acres in Nehasane Park, Beech, Maple, Ash, Cherry, and Balsam are mentioned as occurring on Spruce

PLATE IX.

FIG. 1. A HARDWOOD RIDGE. WHITNEY PRESERVE.

FIG. 2. A TYPICAL HARDWOOD FOREST, WITH UNDERGROWTH OF YOUNG BEECH AND MAPLE AND SCATTERING WITCH HOBBLE AND MOOSEWOOD.

slopes. The acres were measured off in strips, and in consequence it was frequently necessary to include small patches in other situations which contain a larger proportion of these species than the typical Spruce slopes.

Acre measurements (average of 271 acres) on Spruce slopes.

[From "The Adirondack Spruce."]

(Average number of trees per acre, percentage in mixture, and average and maximum diameters of all sound trees 10 inches and over in diameter breast high.)

Name of species.	Average number of trees per acre.	Percentage of each species.	Average diameter breast high.	Maximum diameter breast high.
			Inches.	Inches.
Spruce	34.90	48.45	12.90	34
Birch	13.79	19.52	18.60	40
Beech	7.20	10.26	13.10	27
Hard Maple	4.00	5.70	14.00	31
Hemlock	5.20	7.42	16.30	42
Balsam	3.20	4.56	11.40	18
Soft Maple	2.50	3.56	13.70	25
White Pine	.30	.42	21.90	42
Ash	.01	.02	12.70	14
Cherry	.06	.09	14.20	20
Average of all species	70.17	100.00	14.88	29.3
Average of all species except Spruce	36.17	51.55	15.10	28.8

DISTRIBUTION OF THE FOREST TYPES.

The types of forest described above are found throughout the section included in this working plan. The proportion of each type varies, however, greatly in different sections. In Nehasane Park the distribution was determined to be about as follows:

	Per cent.
Swamp land	25
Spruce flats	10
Hardwood land	40
Spruce slopes	25

It has been shown that the topography of the Whitney Preserve is different from that in Nehasane Park in that there are fewer small ridges with steep slopes and a greater amount of level and rolling land. The following rough estimate was made from a rapid examination of the area:

	Per cent.
Swamp land	20
Spruce flats	30
Hardwood land	40
Spruce slopes	10

In the study of the Spruce in Nehasane Park in 1897 measurements were taken of 1,046 acres. In the next table the average number of trees, percentage in mixture, and average and maximum diameter of all sound trees over 10 inches in diameter on these sample plots are shown. A table prepared from a similar study of the forest in the Whitney Preserve would vary somewhat on account of the different proportion of the forest types, but the difference would not be great enough to warrant the expense of making such a study.

Acre measurements (average of 1,046 acres) at Nehasane Park.

[From " The Adirondack Spruce."]

(Average number of trees per acre, percentage in mixture, and average and maximum diameters of all sound trees 10 inches and over in diameter breast high.)

Name of species.	Average number of trees per acre.	Percentage of each species.	Average diameter breast high.	Maximum diameter breast high.
			Inches.	Inches.
Spruce	31.40	42.77	13.0	30
Birch	14.09	19.06	17.1	38
Beech	10.00	13.62	13.2	26
Hard Maple	6.10	8.30	13.9	30
Hemlock	4.60	6.26	16.7	37
Balsam	4.20	5.72	11.4	20
Soft Maple	2.60	3.54	13.6	28
White Pine	.18	.24	18.4	30
Ash	.16	.22	12.9	19
Cedar	.12	.16	14.5	28
Cherry	.08	.11	15.3	24
Average of all species	73.44	100.00	14.5	29
Average of all species except Spruce	42.04	57.23	14.7	28.9

SPECIAL CONSIDERATION OF THE SPRUCE.

HABIT.

In favorable localities and in crowded forests the Spruce forms a long, clear, full bole, and a rather compact, short, and blunted crown. It attains in Nehasane Park a height of 100 feet and a diameter of 34 inches. These dimensions are, however, rare, and the average for large trees is not over 90 feet in height, and, for the diameter, from 24 to 26 inches. On low, swampy ground Spruce has a long crown, and is comparatively short. The average length of crown for all situations and soils is about 40 feet, and the average clear length from 25 to 30 feet. The average length of the merchantable log was found to be 46 feet. The root system is flat and superficial, and the tree, in consequence, is able to thrive on shallow soils.

Spruce reaches a great age in the Adirondacks, the largest trees being from 200 to 300 years old. The average age of trees of different sizes is shown in the following table, which is compiled from the measurements of 283 trees made in Nehasane Park during 1897:

Average age of merchantable Spruce of different diameters.

Diameter breast high.	Trees measured.	Average age.	Diameter breast high.	Trees measured.	Average age.
Inches.	*Number.*	*Years.*	*Inches.*	*Number.*	*Years.*
9	17	163	18	17	219
10	38	165	19	10	228
11	48	171	20	5	229
12	28	184	21	4	231
13	28	186	22	5	236
14	39	206	23	5	253
15	18	199	24	5	255
16	12	217	27	2	310
17	12	211			

SOIL AND SITUATION.

The influence of situation and soil on the character and distribution of the Spruce is very marked. In general, the Spruce may be divided into three classes with fairly distinct lines, according as it is found on hardwood lands or Spruce slopes, on swamp lands or on the intermediate Spruce flats. Occasional groups of Spruce on the narrow tops of high ridges belong also to the latter class. While the character of the tree varies according to the situation, yet the Spruce is not fastidious, for it occupies all situations and soils—the tops of mountains and ridges, abrupt rocky slopes, and low wet swamps, as well as good soil. The best Spruce is found on rich flats or moderate slopes with rich fresh soil. Any aspect is good if the soil is suitable. It must not be wet or acid. Thus the largest Spruce is found on low, moderate slopes, in sheltered coves, along the benches or hollows of steep slopes, and on rich flats. On low, swampy land it is short and of slow growth. Spruce of intermediate growth occurs on Spruce flats, where the soil is fresh, or even moist, but not wet.

Aside from these general considerations the presence or absence of the Spruce in certain places is determined chiefly by accidental distribution and by the struggle with other species for possession of the ground. On steep southwestern slopes it is found in great abundance, and sometimes almost pure. This is not because the soil and aspect are here most favorable to the growth of Spruce, but because many of the hardwoods will not grow on such rocky, thin soil, and the Spruce is thus left almost without competitors. In the same way Spruce often predominates on poor, low, moist, or even wet lands, because in such places, also, it is almost without competition. Spruce is then most abundant, not necessarily where the situation and soil are best suited to

4364—No. 26 ——3

its development, but in many cases where the soil is so poor that no other tree will grow. It is most abundant on the brows of ridges, on knolls, steep slopes, along the edges of lakes, and often on moist ground. On high land it must contend with the numerous and persistent hardwoods, which, in capacity to bear shade, in height growth, and in reproductive capacity, are fully equal to it.

TOLERANCE.

The fact that young seedlings and small trees are so widely distributed through the forest is due in part to the ability of this tree to grow under shade. This does not mean that the Spruce will not flourish in the light, but merely that it is tolerant of the heavy cover which is a distinguishing characteristic of the hardwood forest in the Adirondacks and throughout New England. Specimens from 100 to 150 years old, and less than 6 inches in diameter, are common. Such trees have survived on the sunlight which could penetrate the heavy crowns above them, and, although not in vigorous health, are capable of continuing the struggle to an advanced age. This ability to tolerate heavy shade is common to large numbers of forest trees, among which both the Beech and the Hard Maple excel the Spruce in this regard. But few trees possess the wonderful capacity of the Spruce to recover from long years of suppression and grow almost or quite as vigorously and rapidly after it is ended as though all the conditions of life had been favorable from the beginning. It is to this capacity more than any other that the Spruce owes its presence in the Adirondack forests. Slow of growth in youth, and germinating for the most part under heavy shade, the Spruce could not survive in the hardwood forest, where it reaches its best development, except by the combination of these two qualities— the ability to bear shade and the power to flourish vigorously when the suppression is over. (Pl. X, fig. 1.)

This power of tolerance is not restricted to early life, although very marked at that time, but continues into age as well. Thus, in Nehasane Park several trees but 9 inches in diameter were found to have more than 200 annual rings on the stump, and of eighteen Spruces with diameters ranging from 8.5 to 9.4 inches, but seven were younger than 150 years, and none were younger than 100 years. One Spruce stump 4.5 inches in diameter had 121 annual rings. These trees had grown for years crowded and shaded by their more thrifty neighbors. Under such circumstances it is common to find small trees still alive, but with flattened and umbrella-shaped crowns (Pl. X, fig. 2). Even such trees are not beyond the possibility of usefulness. If the shade be removed they will usually begin to grow as vigorously as though they had never been suppressed. If the leading shoot has been killed, which is sometimes the case, a side branch will turn upward and take its place, and the growth, although somewhat retarded by the accident, will go rapidly on. A considerable proportion of all the large Red Spruce in

FIG. 1.—A SMALL SPRUCE, ONCE SUPPRESSED, WHICH HAS BEEN GROWING VIGOROUSLY SINCE THE REMOVAL OF THE SHADE.

FIG. 2.—A SMALL SPRUCE WHICH HAS RECOVERED ITS NORMAL RATE OF GROWTH AFTER YEARS OF SUPPRESSION.

From A Primer of Forestry.

the Adirondacks is found on examination to have passed through this umbrella stage. On old windfalls in certain sections, for example, and particularly on low flats, many of the old Spruces carry clusters of very persistent branches growing close together at 10 or 15 feet above the ground. Such branches mark a period when the crown was flattened and umbrella shaped. The present size of these Spruces shows plainly how, when the old trees above them were blown down, they shot up and grew thriftily in spite of the severe circumstances of their youth. It is true that when trees have attained such a size before being set free the injury to the lumber is serious, for the persistent branches entail the loss of a certain amount of clear stuff. If, however, the tree is small when freed, the knots from which these branches grew may be covered over in time, and lumber of good quality may be produced.

REPRODUCTION.

Before determining upon a system of conservative lumbering, a thorough study must be made of the reproduction of the forest; and before advising the owner to leave trees of merchantable size to reseed the openings made in lumbering, there must be a certainty that this purpose will be accomplished. In the present case a strong factor in favor of leaving all trees under 10 rather than only those under 8 inches in diameter is that there will be a greater number of seed trees, and it is proposed, further, to leave a large number of trees over 10 inches in diameter to supplement this amount. (See page 67.) This means the investment of a certain amount in seed trees. It is, therefore, of the first importance to know just what this will accomplish, and whether the results will justify the investment.

THE PRODUCTION OF SEED.

A certain amount of Spruce seed is produced annually, but the trees bear much more heavily in some years than in others. The seed usually begins to ripen in October. The cones cling to the trees until late in the season, and it is common to find Spruce seed on the surface of the late snows in February and March. The seed is light and winged, and is carried by the wind to great distances. The most conspicuous examples of this are seen on high, precipitous mountains which have been burned and which in time have become completely reseeded to Spruce. The complete restocking of the south slope of Salmon Mountain is a case in point. Here the timber was entirely destroyed many years ago, and there is now an almost impenetrable thicket of Spruce about 6 to 10 feet high. Another striking illustration is the restocking of burned islands where the old Spruce has been destroyed, and the trees which must have borne the seed are not less than one-fourth to one-half mile distant.

It so happened that in 1898 the Spruce bore an unusual amount of fruit. Not only were the large trees loaded with cones, but the small poles, 3 or 4 inches in diameter, bore fruit wherever their crowns were not directly under the shade of some other trees. One specimen 3 inches in diameter and about 15 feet high, which had grown in a crowded stand and had been given a considerable amount of light by the opening of a lumber road, was found heavily loaded with fruit. The writer once found in Franklin County a small Spruce only 15 years old which was bearing cones. This small specimen had, however, grown in an open field. Trees growing in open places always bear fruit earlier in life and more prolifically than those in dense forests, because in the former situations they have more light. They bear also more abundantly on rich than on poor soil. The Germans usually ascribe to trees the greatest capacity to produce seed when their rate of height growth has reached its maximum. In the Adirondacks Spruce begins to bear seed when the crown succeeds in reaching the light, and it begins to bear heavily when the top of the crown thickens. At first a few cones are borne near the main stem below the last year's growth. As the crown thickens and spreads, the cones are borne on the side branches. The period of beginning to bear seed may be delayed till the trees are 80 or 100 years old, for often they are overtopped and do not succeed in growing up into the light before this age. This long suppression does not, however, prevent their producing abundant fruit when the shade is removed. Spruce continues to bear seed to a great age.

The fact that a tree is unsound does not seem to affect its capacity to bear fruit, just as a tree which is unsound may often continue to grow rapidly.

Millions of seeds fall which never germinate. The squirrels and mice eat a considerable number, but probably the majority fail to germinate because of the lack of certain essential conditions.

CONDITIONS NECESSARY FOR REPRODUCTION.

Besides the power of the trees to produce seed, the chief essentials of good reproduction are a favorable germinating bed and a certain amount of light.

The character of the seed bed is determined by the situation and soil, the density of the forest, and by the component species. It makes a great difference in the reproduction of many trees whether there is a layer of hardwood leaves on the surface of the ground, a matting of needles, abundant moss, or no soil covering at all. In dense hardwood forests there is always a heavy layer of leaves, and here Spruce has great difficulty in obtaining a foothold. It delights, however, in moss such as is often found under coniferous trees, but does not thrive as well if the soil is very wet. Spruce seed will germinate well also in a matting of needles or on bare mineral soil.

The density of the forest influences reproduction not only by its effect on the character of the soil cover, but by controlling the degree of light in the forest, a certain amount of which is necessary for the germination and subsequent development of the young trees.

The reproduction of Spruce is often hindered by Witch Hobble. This shrub frequently comes up in considerable quantities on lumbered land, and also in the uncut forest where the density is not great, and sometimes prevents the development of small Spruces by the dense shade of its large leaves. It is found most abundantly on hardwood land.

PURE SPRUCE.

The question is often asked why, in spite of the excellent reproduction of Spruce, the lands on the western slope of the Adirondacks do not yield as heavily as those in the White Mountains of New Hampshire. (Pl. XI, figs. 1 and 2.) The average yield of Spruce in certain sections of the latter region is 10,000 board feet per acre, while in the Adirondacks a yield of 4,000 feet is considered large. The reason is not that the Adirondack land is less productive, but that there is a greater amount of hardwood timber in mixture. When the two regions are compared, however, it will be found that the laws governing the distribution of the trees are identical, and that the reasons for a larger amount of hardwoods in the Adirondacks lie in the difference in topography. The western slope of the Adirondacks may be described as a high plateau broken into hills, ridges, and knolls, interspersed with lakes, swamps, and flats. Those sections of the White Mountains where the yield of the Spruce is so great are characterized by high mountains. Much of the timber land is, in consequence, on the long steep slopes of the high ridges where the soil is thin and unsuited to the growth of the hardwoods. There are, however, many high flats covered with Spruce, on which the soil is deep enough to admit hardwood trees. Here the Spruce predominates chiefly because it has succeeded in occupying the ground first and the hardwoods have been excluded. Such conditions are exactly duplicated in the western Adirondacks on limited tracts, and in such places the Spruce is dense and the yield large. Spruce occurs pure, therefore, either in sections where hardwood trees have difficulty in growing, or where, through some accidental circumstances, it has succeeded in establishing itself before any other species. For the first reason it is found chiefly on steep slopes and in rough situations, and for the second reason on Spruce flats and swamps where the old timber has been destroyed by fire or wind, and Spruce happened to spring up more abundantly than other trees.

In the Adirondacks the patches of pure Spruce are usually composed of comparatively young trees. The reason for this is that the situations where pure stands are found are exposed to windfall. Thus, on the slopes which face the dangerous wind, on the thin soil of Spruce flats, and in the moist swamps, windfall is common, and the timber is usually blown down before it reaches maturity. After a tract of land has been cleared by wind, fire, or otherwise, the succeeding growth is of a comparatively even age. Seed is distributed over the clearing, and the whole area stocked with some kind of tree growth in a comparatively short time. After a windfall there are usually a few saplings which have escaped being blown down, but aside from these few specimens the second growth often will not vary more than 10 to 20 years in age. This new growth frequently comes up very dense, as many as 4,000 or 5,000 plants often springing up on 1 acre. As these small trees grow larger and require more light and space for their development, the more thrifty plants take the lead and overtop the weak specimens, which die on account of the shade. As the trees grow older their number falls off, but because of the great ability of the Spruce to tolerate shade there is always a large number of trees per acre in a pure forest. On account of the mutual crowding of the trees the lower branches die and break off early in life, and as a result long, clear shafts are produced.

From a large number of measurements in the heavy Spruce forests in the White Mountains of New Hampshire, it was found that from 200 to 250 trees often grow on 1 acre at maturity.

SPRUCE IN MIXTURE.

In a virgin forest of mixed species, like that in the Adirondacks, the life history of the Spruce is entirely different from that in pure stands. Here large tracts are seldom cleared by destructive natural agencies, but individual trees are continually dying and being replaced by others, so that the forest is composed of trees of all sizes and ages. In the technical parlance of forestry such a stand is called a "selection" forest. It is obvious that the young trees which germinate in openings made by the death of one or two trees will have comparatively little light for their development. The consequence is that the young Spruce which comes up under such conditions is very backward in its growth and survives only through its marvelous capacity to live in deep shade. If the crowns of the larger trees close together above the small trees, the growth in height is frequently so checked that the terminal shoots add but a fraction of an inch each year. In such cases the growth goes chiefly to the side branches, with the result that the trees are shaped like mushrooms. (Pl. X, fig. 2.) When the cover is removed from overhead the young trees shoot up with new vigor and attain a normal development; but where the side branches are large the timber is apt to be coarse. It has been observed also that trees which have been suppressed in this way are apt to become rotten at the place where the branches are clustered.

In a pure forest, where the trees are of about the same age, the timber grows more rapidly than in a mixed forest, because the competition is between trees of approximately the same height, and in consequence there is no shade from above, as is the case in mixed hardwood forests.

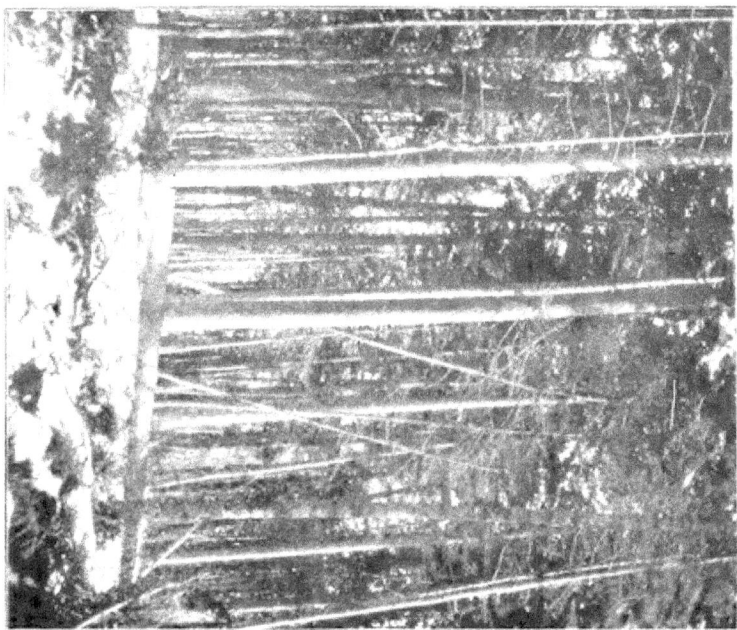

FIG. 1. HEAVY SPRUCE TIMBER. MAD RIVER, NEW HAMPSHIRE.

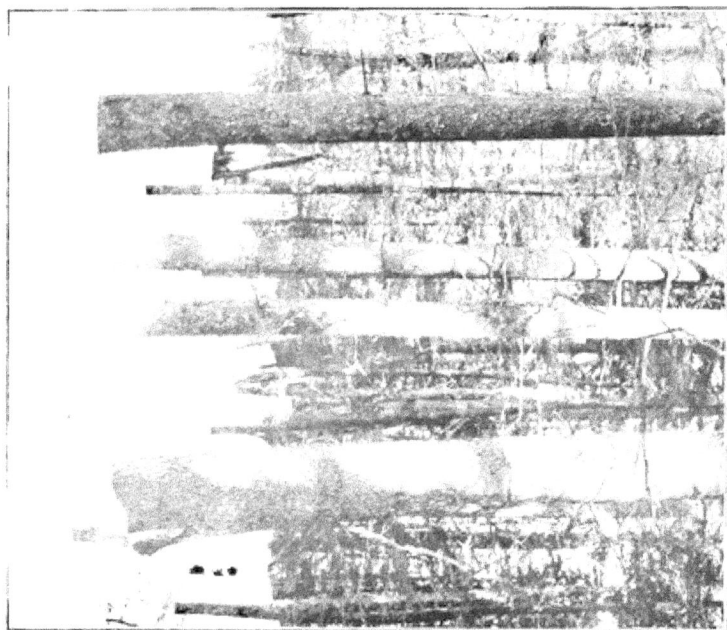

FIG. 2.—NEARLY PURE SPRUCE. MAD RIVER, NEW HAMPSHIRE.

While the Spruce grows more rapidly and produces straighter and clearer timber in pure forests, the danger from windfall is much greater than where there is a scattering of Birch or other hardwood timber. The best results are obtained where the hardwoods form about one-quarter of the crop.

As is explained on page 36, the reproduction of Spruce is better in pure than in mixed forests, because there are no seed trees of other species in the immediate neighborhood, and in consequence there is but little competition for the occupancy of the ground, and also because the soil cover is more favorable to the germination of Spruce seed.

THE GROWTH OF SPRUCE.

EFFECT OF THINNING.

It has been found that when a crowded stand is thinned the trees which remain grow more rapidly than before. This accelerated growth is caused, first, by the more rapid disintegration of the humus and the consequent liberation of an increased amount of available food material, and, second, by the increased spread and efficiency of the roots and crowns.

In the Adirondacks, where the forest is dense and the climate cool, a deep layer of humus accumulates. When the forest is thinned the humus disintegrates more rapidly on account of the admission of the sun's rays and the freer circulation of air, and an increased amount of food material is made available for the growth of the trees. The immediate increase in growth is probably due to this cause. How long it will last depends upon the length of time before the humus disappears. Professor Hartig, of Munich, estimates this period, under favorable conditions, at about 10 years.

The effect of openings in the forest on vigorous and suppressed trees alike is to give them more room for development, a larger and better apparatus of roots and leaves for gathering and digesting food, and so to increase their rate of growth in diameter and height.

The practice of thinning is based on this capacity for increased growth on the part of trees which have been more or less vigorously set free, or, in other words, on the part of the members of a piece of forest which has been thinned. The removal of a certain number of trees from overcrowded woods increases the final product, instead of decreasing it, and an additional product is obtained from the wood cut in the thinning. In this way the total output of a piece of forest in final cuttings and thinnings together is greater than it would be without sylvicultural attention.

INCREASED GROWTH AFTER LUMBERING.

In the Adirondacks the forest to be dealt with does not consist of one species, but is a mixture of deciduous and coniferous trees of all ages. The cutting there has been governed by the distribution of merchantable timber, and such considerations as have just been described have been left entirely out of account. In this way it happens that a considerable amount of old Spruce may be removed with very little benefit to the young trees of that species. Old Birch and Maple and other hardwoods may remain, and the effect of the cutting may not be to free any considerable number of young Spruce trees from the heavy cover overhead. In other cases the merchantable Spruce may stand in groups of old trees without young growth, so that their removal will have little or no effect on the young trees which remain. The best results are attained only when the timber removed was well distributed above the young trees. Where but a single merchantable species is cut from the mixed forest this can not often be the case. Just what the effect of the cutting will be on the remaining trees depends then on the character of all the species in mixture as well as on the number and distribution of the old trees which were removed. It is therefore difficult to reach figures more than approximately exact.

The following method of study was employed as a means of attacking this question: On areas of definite size, usually of 1 acre each, on cut-over land, all trees which would make pulp wood were cut and analyzed so that their exact contents were known. The stumps and tops of trees taken at the first cut, and the distance between them, were then measured, and the number of logs and the amount of timber removed at that time were thus closely ascertained. All trees left by the second cut were then carefully measured with callipers. The date of the first cut was known, and it served, together with the measurements and counting of rings carried out in the second cut, to reestablish the history of the stand for about 30 years back. Fourteen such small plots were laid off, and over 2,000 trees were carefully analyzed. The valuation surveys which were carried out upon them are found in detail in the appendix of "The Adirondack Spruce."

The object in taking these stem-analyses was to determine the present rate of growth in diameter of trees of all sizes and to obtain measurements of enough trees to make volume tables (or tables of solid contents). The stem-analyses were, therefore, not as complete as would have been the case had the intention been to make tables of growth according to the German methods.

The following measurements were taken of each tree:

Diameter at 4.5 feet from the ground.

Diameter on the stump inside and outside the bark.

Diameter at the top of each log inside and outside the bark.

Height of stump.

Length of each log and of the top.

The rings were counted on the stump and at the upper end of each log for 30 years in from the bark, and the distance to each 10-year point was measured. From these measurements it was easy to determine which trees had increased in rapidity of growth after the lumbering and which had not.

Other measurements were taken, but, as they did not contribute directly to the results here presented, no further mention of them is required.

The great labor involved in collecting such data made it impossible to extend the above-mentioned inquiry beyond the 2,000 trees analyzed. This number, however, is great enough to establish a trustworthy basis, and the figures derived from it are used as such in the present study. The reasonableness of these figures, their number, and the fact that the effect of the probable removal of hardwoods from Spruce lands during the next few years has been neglected, combined to give assurance that any error resulting from their use will be in favor of the forest owner, not against him.

The following table gives the percentage of small trees whose growth was found to have been increased by the cutting of the old timber. It will be noticed that the causes of irregularity mentioned above have acted so powerfully as to prevent the statement of any exact ratio between the percentage of trees affected and the amount of timber removed. In general the former may be taken at about 20 per cent.

Amount of timber in standards removed at first cutting, and percentage of small trees left standing whose growth was accelerated, on fourteen sample plots at Santa Clara, N. Y.

[From " The Adirondack Spruce."]

Area of sample plot.	Amount removed at first cutting.	Small trees whose growth was accelerated.	Area of sample plot.	Amount removed at first cutting.	Small trees whose growth was accelerated.
Acres.	Standards.	Per cent.	Acres.	Standards.	Per cent.
0.8	38.4	42	1.0	10.0	36
1.0	17.0	31	1.0	9.8	11
.9	14.2	6	.2	4.4	21
1.0	14.0	40	1.0	4.2	11
1.0	13.0	13	1.0	2.6	.5
1.5	11.8	.2	1.0	1.5	....
1.5	11.2	20	1.0	.5	....

The area chosen for the study just described was at Santa Clara, Franklin County, N. Y. Here the first lumbering operations took place in 1882, the next in 1888 and 1891, and the final crop was removed in 1896. In 1882 probably only the largest and best trees were taken, and in consequence the number cut was small. At least it was not possible to find any small trees showing an increased growth beginning at that date. The cuttings of 1888 and 1891 were much closer, and the effect on the small trees was very marked.

In most cases the increased growth began with the first season after the cutting. On the areas cut over in 1888 there were but a few trees which showed an accelerated growth beginning after that year. In these cases it was not possible to determine whether the new start had been delayed, or whether it was due to windfalls following the cutting. On the area cut over in 1891 a considerable number of trees showed a small increase in growth the first year, and a much more rapid increase the following years. In general, it may be said that the increased growth takes place, as a rule, the first year, and that it will in all probability continue until the next cutting, for if the first cause (the rapid decomposition of the humus) ceases after a few years, the roots and crowns will have begun to spread, and the second cause will thus have come into operation.

The average rate of growth in diameter on the stump of 1,593 trees is found in the table following. It was determined for all the trees together for the periods just before and after the previous cutting, and separately for those whose growth was accelerated. These trees occurred on eleven of the sample plots which were studied at Santa Clara. The other three plots were omitted because only a very few trees were taken at the first cut, and almost none of the remaining small trees showed accelerated growth. These measurements exhibit the rate of growth under various conditions of situation and soil.

The figures of diameter growth given in the table were derived from measurements of the last ten rings. For example, the third column gives the average rate of growth of all trees just before the last cutting, and was found in each case by subtracting the increment for the period since lumbering from the increment for the last 10 years, and dividing by the number of years during which the growth thus ascertained was made. The fifth column gives the average rate of growth of all trees since the lumbering, whether they show an increased growth or not. The column which gives the current annual growth in diameter after the values have been made regular by a curve also requires a word of explanation. When a series of averages are made out it often happens that the successive figures do not follow quite regularly. It will be noticed in the table that this is true of the lower part of the fourth column, and that it is probably explained by the lack of enough trees of 15 inches in diameter to get a fair average. In such cases the values are plotted on cross-section paper and a regular curve is drawn through or near the points which represent them. The points through which the curve actually passes are then taken as the true values. In this way accidental irregularities are avoided, and the results are brought much nearer the truth.

Average rate of growth in diameter on the stump of 1,593 trees on cut-over land at Santa Clara, N. Y.

[From "The Adirondack Spruce."]

(Total number trees, 1,593. Number trees showing increased growth, 294, or 18 per cent.)

Diameter.	Number of trees.	Current annual growth in diameter just before first cutting.	Current annual growth in diameter since first cutting.	Current annual growth in diameter cutting (values made regular by a curve).	Number of years required to grow 1 inch in diameter.	Trees showing increased growth.	
						Number.	Current annual growth in diameter since first cutting.
Inches.		Inches.	Inches.	Inches.			Inches.
5	8	0.005	0.095	0.09	11	1	0.10
6	158	.08	.10	.10	10	16	.18
7	329	.09	.11	.109	9	63	.185
8	350	.105	.125	.125	8	77	.205
9	277	.12	.14	.14	7	59	.205
10	226	.135	.15	.15	7	50	.215
11	135	.13	.145	.16	7	18	.21
12	64	.165	.175	.17	6	7	.24
13	30	.165	.17	.178	6	2	.17
14	11	.15	.15	.185	6	1	.20
15	1	.08	.08	.192	6	....	....
16	4	.20	.20	.20	5	....	....
Average........		.112	.157	....	....	....	.20
No. years to grow 1 inch..........		9	....	....	7	....	5

GROWTH IN THE ORIGINAL FOREST.

It is interesting to compare the growth in diameter of trees growing in the original forest with the figures just given for cut-over land. Stem analyses were made on 298 trees in original forest near Nehasane, from which the table given below has been compiled. These measurements were taken at a lumber job on the southern edge of Nehasane Park and on the Brandreth tract.

Rate of growth in diameter for the last 10 years, from measurements of 298 trees in Nehasane Park.

[From "The Adirondack Spruce."]

Number of trees.	Diameter.	Mean annual growth in diameter.	Number of years required to grow 1 inch.	Number of trees.	Diameter.	Mean annual growth in diameter.	Number of years required to grow 1 inch.
	Inches.	Inches.			Inches.	Inches.	
18	9	0.10	10	11	19	0.12	8
39	10	.12	8	5	20	.10	10
48	11	.14	7	4	21	.11	9
28	12	.12	8	5	22	.08	12
29	13	.13	8	5	23	.10	10
39	14	.14	7	5	24	.10	10
19	15	.11	9	2	27	.14	7
12	16	.11	9				
12	17	.11	9	Average......		.122	8
17	18	.11	9				

GROWTH IN DIFFERENT PARTS OF A TREE.

An exceedingly interesting question is the rate of growth of different parts of the same tree. It must be borne in mind that the material for growth is elaborated within the crown from material derived from the air and the roots, and that this elaborated sap comes down in the inside of the bark. It is not difficult to see that within the crown the rate of growth must be more rapid at the lower part than near the top, because each branch adds a certain amount of material for the growth below which the stem above did not have. In general, except close to the ground, the growth falls off below the crown. In the case of trees very much suppressed it may happen that not enough material for growth is formed in the crown to reach the lower part of the stem, and in some cases the number of annual rings on the stump will not represent accurately the age of the tree, because for some years there may have been no growth whatever in the lower part of the stem. This happens, however, usually only in the case of dying trees. The width of the annual rings is smaller at the lower part of the stem than above, even if the same amount of material is brought down, because it has to extend over a larger surface. The results of the measurements taken on about 2,000 Spruces show the largest growth in the crown, the smallest at the top of the first log, and a medium growth on the stump. Where the trees had an increased growth after thinning, the largest growth was at the stump. The fact that the increased growth at this part of the stem is out of proportion to that above has led some observers to believe that it is not necessary for all the food materials to be digested in the crown before they can be used in growth. This theory is the result of the phenomenon just mentioned, and of the fact that those roots of a tree which are in the richest soil grow to the largest size. In order to present more clearly the relation of the rate of growth at the different parts of the tree under the new influences of light and space after thinning, the following table has been made from 59 trees, all of which showed accelerated growth on the stump:

Rate of growth at different sections of the stem.
[From "The Adirondack Spruce."]
(Mean annual diameter growth.)

Diameter.	On the stump.		Top of first log.		Top of second log.		Number of trees.
	1886-1888	1888-1896	1886-1888	1888-1896	1886-1888	1888-1896	
Inches.							
6	0.14	0.20	0.12	0.12	....	....	1
7	.105	.24	.12	.14	0.15	0.16	12
8	.125	.20	.12	.15	.16	.20	12
9	.11	.20	.11	.12	.14	.16	15
10	.13	.21	.11	.16	.15	.22	10
11	.105	.17	.10	.11	.12	.16	5
12	.17	.23	.08	.14	.20	.22	4
Average.	.12	.21	.11	.13	.15	.18	59

NOTE.—The above results make it clear that measurements taken at the top of the first or second log can not safely be used in reasoning about growth on the stump, or vice versa.

THE PRODUCTION OF SPRUCE.

In the study of the production of a forest it is necessary to know not only the rate of growth of the individual trees, but also how much young timber will be left standing after lumbering to form the basis for a second crop. An exhaustive study of this question was made in the investigation of the Spruce in Nehasane Park in 1897. In this connection 1,046 sample plots, of 1 acre each, were surveyed to determine the number of trees per acre of different diameters. The results of these measurements are summarized in the table following. The surveys are grouped according as the yield per acre was, in round numbers, 1,000, 2,000, 3,000, etc., board feet. In each class the total number of acres involved is stated, and the average number of trees per acre. For the sake of accuracy, fractions of trees have been given. In the case of the large diameters there is less than one tree of each diameter per acre, and the result is often a very small fraction.

Average number of trees per acre of different diameters, and number of acres measured, classified according to the yield in board feet of all trees 10 inches and over in diameter breast high.

[From "The Adirondack Spruce."]

Diameter breast high.	Yield of all trees 10 inches and over in diameter breast high, in board feet.											
	1,000 (139 acres).	2,000 (213 acres).	3,000 (223 acres).	4,000 (204 acres).	5,000 (106 acres).	6,000 (71 acres).	7,000 (37 acres).	8,000 (21 acres).	9,000 (4 acres).	10,000 (5 acres).	11,000 (1 acre).	12,000 (2 acres).
	Average number of trees.											
Inches.												
2	22.30	20.50	21.10	21.20	21.50	24.90	26.30	24.20	21.50	23.00	16.0	49.0
3	18.70	19.30	20.00	19.10	19.90	23.30	24.30	24.10	18.20	24.40	9.0	41.0
4	17.90	18.10	18.20	18.30	19.70	21.40	23.10	21.80	14.50	18.10	20.0	34.0
5	12.80	13.00	12.90	13.90	14.60	16.90	18.40	18.50	13.00	17.80	15.0	23.5
6	10.90	10.60	12.10	12.20	13.60	13.60	14.50	13.20	13.00	16.00	25.0	17.5
7	8.70	8.30	9.20	10.20	10.60	11.90	12.80	12.90	12.70	12.00	17.0	19.5
8	6.80	7.40	7.80	8.20	8.90	9.70	10.00	9.80	11.00	8.40	20.0	13.5
9	5.30	5.40	6.50	7.50	7.30	8.80	10.30	9.40	7.20	8.60	10.0	13.0
10	4.60	5.30	6.80	6.90	7.80	8.70	9.80	9.60	11.00	8.20	8.0	14.0
11	3.20	3.80	4.60	5.50	6.50	6.80	9.60	7.40	8.50	8.60	12.0	15.0
12	2.10	3.60	4.10	5.20	5.60	6.60	7.80	6.40	7.20	8.60	18.0	17.0
13	1.40	2.60	3.60	4.20	4.70	5.10	6.40	7.10	7.50	6.00	13.0	14.0
14	1.30	1.90	2.80	3.50	4.40	5.10	6.30	5.80	7.00	6.40	12.0	8.0
15	.90	1.50	2.40	3.30	3.80	4.00	4.00	4.90	6.20	7.00	4.0	7.5
16	.50	1.20	1.80	2.40	2.60	2.90	3.30	4.10	7.00	4.20	5.0	5.0
17	.00	.90	1.30	1.80	2.40	2.20	3.00	2.30	4.00	5.60	2.0	6.0
18	.30	.60	1.00	1.20	1.80	1.90	2.00	2.20	3.20	3.20	2.0	2.5
19	.20	.40	.60	.80	1.00	1.20	1.10	1.30	1.70	2.40	1.0	2.0
20	.20	.30	.40	.50	.70	.80	.90	1.10	1.50	2.00	2.0	1.0
21	.08	.20	.20	.40	.50	.60	.60	1.00	1.70	1.20	1.0	1.5
22	.04	.20	.20	.20	.20	1.30	1.30	1.00	1.20	.50	....	....
23	.02	.10	.20	.10	.20	.10	.20	.30	1.20	.40	....	....
24	....	.03	.07	.10	.03	.07	.10	.10	.70	.40	....	....
25	.01	.04	.03	.02	.04	.03	.03	.10	.20	.20	....	....
26	....	.02	.01	.03	.01	.03	.03	.10	....	....	....	.5
27	....	....	.01	.01	....	.06	.03	.05	....	....	....	
28	.01	....	.01	....	....	.01	....					
30	....	....	.004	....	....	....						
31	....	....	.004	....	....							
34	....	....	....	....	.01	....						

YIELD TABLES.

The material given in the preceding tables was prepared for the purpose of predicting future crops of timber after cutting to a given limit on lands yielding a known amount of Spruce. It is of great importance to the landowner to know how soon he can return to a certain tract of land after cutting and obtain the same yield as at first, and to what minimum diameter it will be most profitable in the long run to cut. There can be no doubt that the best immediate returns are obtained by cutting down to 5 inches. Forest management is out of the question for the lumberman who wishes to make all the money possible out of his property at once and without regard to its value in the future, for it rests on the premise that forest land is so much productive capital and that its productive capacity should not be impaired. It is easy to show that, if the Spruce is cut down to 5 inches, so long a time must elapse before there will be merchantable Spruce on the area again that it will not pay to hold the land for the next crop. In such a case there would be no timber worth cutting even for pulp in less than 50 to 75 years. Interest charges, taxes, and the cost of production can not be met for the sake of so meager a crop as would result from the present system of cutting at the end of that period.

Many lumbermen are now cutting, from lands lumbered 10, 15, or 20 years ago, a yield as large as the first cut. As a rule they are cutting to a smaller diameter than at first, as, for example, in some cases where the first cut was to about 10 inches the second cut is removing everything down to 5 inches. Even where the limit is said to have been the same at both cuts and the product the same, it must be remembered that, while no trees may have been taken under 10 inches at either cut, many trees over 10 inches, which would now be merchantable, at the time of the first cut were considered unfit for market. Nor is it probable that the cutting to the limit at first was as close as it would be now.

The yield tables have been made in order to give definite information as to the production of cut-over Spruce lands. They embody the results of measurements on 1,046 test acres, classified according as the yield was nearest 1,000, 2,000, 3,000 board feet, etc., per acre.

In the tables, as given in "The Adirondack Spruce," there were stated the number of acres in each class, the exact average yield of these acres, and the amount of timber which would be obtained in 10, 20, and 30 years after cutting down to 10, 12, and 14 inches. The number of years which must elapse before the land will yield exactly the same amount as at the first cut was also shown. These tables are given in the Appendix.

In working with the above-mentioned tables during the past year it was found that they could be used more conveniently if the predicted yield in 10, 20, and 30 years were expressed in percentage of the original stand as well as in board feet, and if the amount of timber 12 and 14 inches and over in diameter were expressed in percentage of the stand of trees 10 inches and over. The tables would have a further advantage if these values were determined for acres yielding exactly 1,000, 2,000, 3,000, etc., board feet per acre, instead of for acres yielding these amounts in round numbers. Thus for acres which yielded in round numbers 1,000 board feet the actual stand was 1,416 feet. The predicted yield at different decades was, therefore, really determined for acres of 1,416, and not of exactly 1,000, board feet. The tables were reconstructed to show the predicted yields in percentage of the original stands, and the amount of timber 12 and 14 inches and over in diameter, in percentage of the stand of trees 10 inches and over, all values being calculated for acres yielding exactly 1,000, 2,000, 3,000, etc., board feet.[1]

Present yield per acre of Spruce, amount which can be cut in 10, 20, and 30 years after lumbering, and the number of years which must elapse before the same amount can be obtained again, cutting down to 10, 12, and 14 inches.

A.—SPRUCE PER ACRE 10 INCHES AND OVER IN DIAMETER BREAST HIGH.

Yield of all trees 10 inches and over in diameter, breast high, in board feet.	Number of acres measured.	Second cut after 10 years.		Second cut after 20 years.		Second cut after 30 years.		Interval required between equal cuts, in years.
		Percentage of first cut.	Board feet.	Percentage of first cut.	Board feet.	Percentage of first cut.	Board feet.	
1	2	3	4	5	6	7	8	9
1,000	130	20	200	60	600	140	1,400	27
2,000	213	15	300	43	860	94	1,880	32
3,000	223	11	330	41	1,230	70	2,100	36
4,000	204	9	360	35	1,400	56	2,240	39
5,000	106	8	400	33	1,650	50	2,500	41
6,000	71	7	420	32	1,920	46	2,760	43
7,000	37	7	490	30	2,100	42	2,940	45
8,000	21	6	480	27	2,160	37	2,960	47
9,000	4	5	450	24	2,160	32	2,880	49
10,000	5	4	400	21	2,100	27	2,700	51

[1] In order to arrive at the future stand after lumbering, for tracts yielding exactly 1,000, 2,000 feet, etc., per acre, the following method of interpolation was used: On the horizontal lines of cross-section paper there were laid off the different yields per acre in board feet, and on the vertical lines the future yield in periods of 10, 20, and 30 years. Normal curves were drawn through the points of intersection, and the values for acres yielding exactly 1,000, 2,000, etc., feet were ascertained by interpolation. The same method was used to determine the stand of trees 12 and 14 inches and over for acres yielding exactly 1,000, 2,000, 3,000 feet, etc., and also for the intervals required between equal cuts.

Present yield per acre of Spruce, amount which can be cut in 10, 20, and 30 years after lumbering, and the number of years which must elapse before the same amount can be obtained again, cutting down to 10, 12, and 14 inches—Continued.

B.—SPRUCE PER ACRE 12 INCHES AND OVER IN DIAMETER BREAST HIGH.

Yield of all trees 10 inches and over in diameter, breast high, in board feet.	Yield of all trees 12 inches and over in diameter, breast high.		Second cut after 10 years.		Second cut after 20 years.		Second cut after 30 years.		Interval required between equal cuts, in years.
	Percentage of the yield of trees 10 inches and over.	Board feet.	Percentage of first cut over 12 inches.	Board feet.	Percentage of first cut over 12 inches.	Board feet.	Percentage of first cut over 12 inches.	Board feet.	
1	2	3	4	5	6	7	8	9	10
1,000	76	740	68	503	140	1,036	260	1,924	15
2,000	74	1,480	49	725	93	1,376	180	2,664	21
3,000	83	2,490	38	950	69	1,718	132	3,287	24
4,000	85	3,400	32	1,088	59	2,006	110	3,740	29
5,000	85	4,250	29	1,233	54	2,295	97	4,123	31
6,000	85	5,100	27	1,377	52	2,652	90	4,590	32
7,000	85	5,900	26	1,547	51	3,035	88	3,825	33
8,000	86	6,880	25	1,720	47	3,234	82	5,236	35
9,000	87	7,830	24	1,879	41	3,210	72	5,642	36
10,000	87	8,700	21	1,827	34	2,958	60	5,638	38

C.—SPRUCE PER ACRE 14 INCHES AND OVER IN DIAMETER BREAST HIGH.

Yield of all trees 10 inches and over in diameter, breast high, in board feet.	Yield of all trees 14 inches and over in diameter, breast high.		Second cut after 10 years.		Second cut after 20 years.		Interval required between equal cuts, in years.
	Percentage of the yield of trees 14 inches and over.	Board feet.	Percentage of first cut over 14 inches.	Board feet.	Percentage of first cut over 14 inches.	Board feet.	
1	2	3	4	5	6	7	8
1,000	53	530	82	435	160	848	13
2,000	57	1,140	70	798	136	1,550	16
3,000	61	1,830	57	1,043	114	2,086	19
4,000	64	2,560	46	1,179	96	2,456	21
5,000	66	3,300	43	1,419	90	2,970	21
6,000	66	3,960	42	1,663	87	3,505	21
7,000	67	4,690	41	1,923	84	3,940	21
8,000	68	5,440	39	2,122	78	4,243	22
9,000	68	6,120	36	2,203	70	4,284	24
10,000	69	6,900	33	2,277	64	4,416	26

APPLICATION OF THE YIELD TABLES.

In order to show the character of the problems which can be worked out by the yield tables, six examples are given mainly as they appear in "The Adirondack Spruce" to illustrate the reconstructed tables. The application of the tables to Nehasane Park and the Whitney Preserve is shown on page 65 in connection with the proposed plan of forest work.

EXAMPLE NO. 1.

A man owns 30,000 acres, which yields on an average 3,000 board feet per acre of Spruce 10 inches and over in diameter. To what limit will it be most profitable in the long run for him to cut, how much can be cut annually if he wishes to obtain a sustained annual yield, and how soon can he return to the portion lumbered over the first year and cut the same amount of timber above the same diameter limit as at first?

If the diameter limit is 10 inches, the total stand is 30,000 by 3,000 = 90,000,000 board feet; the same yield can be obtained in 36 years (Table A, column 9); the area lumbered annually will be 30,000 ÷ 36 = 833 acres; the annual cut will be 90,000,000 ÷ 36 = 2,500,000 board feet.

If the diameter limit is 12 inches, the average stand per acre is 83 per cent of the stand of trees 10 inches and over (Table B, column 2), i. e., 2,490, or in round numbers, 2,500 board feet. The total stand is 2,500 by 30,000 = 75,000,000 board feet; the same yield can be obtained in 24 years (Table B, column 10); the area lumbered annually will be 30,000 ÷ 24 = 1,250 acres; the annual cut will be 75,000,000 ÷ 24 = 3,125,000 board feet.

If the diameter limit is 14 inches, the average stand per acre is 61 per cent of the yield of trees 10 inches and over (Table C, column 2), i. e., 1,830, or in round numbers 1,800 board feet. The total stand is 30,000 by 1,800 = 54,000,000 board feet; the same yield can be obtained in 19 years (Table C, column 8); the area lumbered over will be 30,000 ÷ 19 = 1,579 acres; the annual cut will be 54,000,000 ÷ 19 = 2,842,105 board feet.

By comparing these results it appears that, if it is desired to cut an equal amount of timber annually for an indefinite period, the largest yield can be obtained by cutting to a 12-inch limit. The area lumbered annually is about 400 acres greater than if 10 inches were the limit, but the annual cut is 625,000 board feet larger. Lumbering under these conditions would nevertheless be profitable, inasmuch as the average stand per acre for trees 12 inches and over in diameter is about 2,500 board feet.

EXAMPLE NO. 2.

A man owns 1,000 acres, yielding 1,500 board feet of Spruce per acre, 12 inches and over in diameter. To what limit will it be most profitable in the long run to cut if he lumbers the entire tract in one year and how soon can he return for a second cut equal to the first?

See Table B, column 3, for the amount nearest 1,500 board feet. The closest figure is 1,480 feet in the second line. All the desired information will be obtained on this line in the three tables.

If the diameter limit is 10 inches, the average yield is, in round numbers, 2,000 board feet (Table A, column 1). The total stand is 1,000 by 2,000 = 2,000,000 board feet. The same yield can be obtained in 32 years (Table A, column 9).

If the diameter limit is 12 inches, the average stand per acre is 1,500 board feet. (See above.) The total stand is 1,000 by 1,500 = 1,500,000 board feet. The same cut can be obtained in 21 years (Table B, column 10).

If the diameter limit is 14 inches, the average stand per acre is 1,140, or in round numbers, 1,150 board feet (Table C, column 3). The total stand is 1,000 by 1,150 = 1,150,000 board feet. The same cut can be obtained in 16 years (Table C, column 8).

If 10 inches is the limit, the tract will yield at present 2,000,000, and in 32 years the same amount again, or together, at that time, 4,000,000 feet. If 12 inches is the limit, 1,500,000 board feet can be obtained now, and in 32 years there can be cut 2,664 feet per acre (Table B, column 9) plus 2 years' growth. The latter is equivalent to 2,664 (column 9) minus 1,376 (column 7), divided by 5, or 248. The yield in 32 years is then 2,664 + 248 = 2,912 board feet per acre, or on the whole tract, including the first cut, 4,412,000 board feet. If 14 inches is the limit, 1,150,000 board feet can be cut now, and the same amount every 16 years. In 32 years a total yield of 3,450,000 board feet can be obtained.

It will therefore be most profitable to cut to 12 inches.

EXAMPLE NO. 3.

A man owns 20,000 acres of Spruce land, from which he has cut 6,000 board feet per acre 12 inches and over in diameter. How much can he obtain in 20 years if at that time he cuts to 10 inches?

See Table B, column 3, for the amount nearest 6,000 board feet. It is found in the seventh line. In 20 years there will be about 3,034 feet per acre, cutting down to 12 inches (Table B, column 7). If 10 inches had been made the limit at the original cut, there could have been obtained 7,000 instead of 6,000 board feet per acre (Table B, columns 1 and 3, seventh line). The stand of the trees 10 and 11 inches in diameter should, under careful treatment, remain constant, or 1,000 board feet, which amount should be added to 3,034, making 4,034, or, in round numbers, 4,000 feet.

EXAMPLE NO. 4.

A man owns 10,000 acres of Spruce land, from which he obtained 1,000 board feet per acre, 10 inches and over in diameter, 10 years ago. How soon can he cut the same amount?

See Table A, column 1. In this table 27 years is given as the time in which 1,000 feet can be obtained at the second cut. The land having been lumbered 10 years ago, it will require 17 years more for the required amount to grow.

EXAMPLE NO. 5.

A man cut his Spruce land 20 years ago, getting 1,760 board feet per acre 12 inches and over in diameter. How much can he get now, cutting to 12 inches?

See Table B, column 3, for the amount nearest 1,760. It is found in the second line. The same amount can be taken out in 21 years after the first cut (Table B, column 10). At the present time, therefore, the owner can obtain nearly the amount of his original cut.

EXAMPLE NO. 6.

A man cuts his Spruce land, which yields 3,160 board feet per acre of trees 10 inches and over in diameter, and wishes to lumber a second time in 20 years. How much can he obtain? Answer. Forty-one per cent of the original cut (Table A, column 5), or 1,296 board feet.

IMPORTANT TREES IN MIXTURE.

WHITE PINE.

In the greater part of the Adirondacks the conditions are not favorable for the best development of the White Pine. Individual trees obtain a great size, but the timber is scattered and forms only a small proportion of the entire forest. Moreover, the majority of old trees are unsound and it is usually necessary to discard the first log. The average diameter is about 22 inches, and the height 100 to 120 feet. The largest specimen seen was cut near the shore of Round Pond, township 23. (Pl. XII, figs. 1 and 2.) It measured 55 inches inside the bark on the stump and had a total height of 153 feet. It yielded eight logs and scaled 25 standards.

FIG. 1.—A SKIDWAY CONTAINING FIVE LOGS FROM A PINE 55 INCHES IN DIAMETER.
WHITNEY PRESERVE.

FIG. 2.—A PINE STUMP 55 INCHES IN DIAMETER. WHITNEY PRESERVE.

Most of the White Pine is very old, but occasional young trees are found on the edges of lakes and streams, and in clearings after windfall and fire. On Forked Lake there is a large amount of comparatively young Pine in excellent condition. Another similar tract was seen between Salmon and Little Salmon lakes where there had evidently been a severe windfall, or possibly a fire, and the Pine had come up plentifully. These trees have an estimated age of 150 years and are tall, clear boled, sound, and thrifty.

White Pine is not fastidious regarding soil and situation, for it is found on thin, stony soil, on the brows of steep slopes, on the moist, meager soil of many Spruce flats, and on the sandy shores of lakes. (Pl. VII, fig. 1.) The controlling factors governing its local distribution are a fair degree of light and a favorable seed bed. Compared to most other trees in the Adirondacks, White Pine is intolerant of shade. For this reason it is usually found where openings have been made by wind or fire. The seed germinates best in moss, in thin duff composed of needles, or in bare mineral soil. Where there is a heavy matting of hardwood leaves it reproduces itself poorly. The seed is able to germinate in fairly dense shade, but the young plant requires a considerable amount of light for further development. As a rule, plants which have sprung up in the shade live only about 10 to 15 years, developing a spindling, crooked stem. Where old Pines occur it is common to find these young plants 3 to 5 feet high, dead or dying from lack of light.

White Pine comes up most abundantly after fire or windfall. The history of burned tracts near swamps or lakes is usually as follows: Immediately after the fire White Birch, Poplar, and Bird Cherry occupy the ground. The Spruce and Pine begin to return within a few years, and are able to live under the other trees, whose shade is not heavy. White Birch, Poplar, and Bird Cherry are all short-lived trees, and eventually die, leaving the Pine and Spruce in possession of the ground. White Pine grows more rapidly than Spruce and forms an upper story over it. It does not cast a heavy shade, when not growing pure in dense masses, and the growth of the Spruce is little hindered.

It is a general law that wherever Pine occurs the reproduction of Spruce is good. Even where there are single Pines numbers of young Spruce can usually be found. This fact is of practical value, for where old Pines are cut a considerable opening is inevitably made in the forest. The presence of the small Spruce, however, is a saving factor, for there are usually enough trees to insure good reproduction.

BIRCH.

Yellow Birch is the characteristic hardwood tree in Nehasane Park and the Whitney Preserve. With an average diameter of 15 inches when mature, in some cases it reaches a diameter of 4 feet and a height of 90 to 100 feet. When growing at its best in dense forest it forms a

long. clear. full trunk and a narrow crown. It inhabits a great variety
of soils and situations. but attains its best development on hardwood
flats. Although it occurs on low, marshy ground, Birch avoids wet
swamps, where it is short, scrubby, and unsound. It has a shallow
root system. well adapted to meager, stony soil. and it frequently
appears on bare rocks. spreading its roots over the edge into the soil
below. Seedlings often come up on logs and stumps. so that when
the latter rot away the tree is supported only by its prop-like roots. In
general. the Birch is more abundant on southerly than on northerly
slopes.

Yellow Birch is decidedly tolerant of shade. but not to the same
degree as Hard Maple. Beech, and Spruce. Under dense hardwoods
its seedlings are less abundant than those of Beech or Maple. In openings it springs up abundantly, with a marked tendency to associate in
groups. Birch reproduces itself prolifically. The seed germinates
better on moss-covered soil than where there is a thick layer of leaf
litter. It is frequently abundant in windfalls. Thus, on Spruce flats,
after windfalls. Birch and Soft Maple often form the second growth.
It is common on Spruce slopes.

The average rate of growth was found to be, for the 78 trees measured. 1 inch in diameter in 20 years. Young trees are plentiful. and,
as in the case of Spruce. there is a regular gradation in number of trees
from the small to the large diameters.

BEECH.

The Beech reaches a diameter of nearly 3 feet. and in dense stands
produces a long. clear. smooth trunk and a narrow. compact crown.
In its choice of soil and situation it is moderately fastidious. It
reaches its best development on moderate northeastern slopes, where it
often occurs in nearly pure patches. On high land it is abundant, and
it is found also on Spruce flats, and even in some marshy situations.
It is extremely unsound on low ground, and indeed throughout the
forest the proportion of unsound Beech is large.

It reproduces itself abundantly. Young trees spring up in dense
thickets where the hardwood forest is thinned. and are capable of living under heavy shade.

Compared to other hardwoods, the growth in diameter is fairly rapid.
The average current rate of growth for 16 trees, with an average
diameter of 13 inches. was 1 inch in 13 years.

HARD MAPLE.

Hard Maple reaches a height of 90 to 100 feet and a diameter of
nearly 3 feet. Of Hard Maples over 10 inches in diameter there are
about 6 sound trees per acre, with an average diameter of 14 inches.
In favorable situations these trees form long. clear trunks and narrow,

compact crowns. They grow on high ground in fresh and rather deep soil, but not in swamps, and are most abundant on northerly slopes and high flats.

Hard Maple reproduces itself prolifically, and is tolerant of heavy shade both in youth and in later life. When the hardwood forest is thinned dense thickets of Hard Maple come up, often to the exclusion of all other species.

The growth in diameter under the present conditions is slow. Measurements were taken of 16 trees which averaged 15 inches in diameter, and the average current rate of growth was found to be 1 inch in diameter in 16 years.

HEMLOCK.

The Hemlock is found in all parts of the two preserves, but reaches its best development on the borders of streams and on the low flats above the swamps. In such situations it is usually more sound than when growing on high slopes and ridges, although in general its timber is of inferior quality and suffers severely from wind shake. On the 1,046 acres measured in Nehasane Park, there were 4 Hemlock trees over 10 inches in diameter per acre, with an average diameter of 17.5 inches.

Hemlock is very tolerant of shade both in youth and in later life, but in the Adirondacks it is inferior in this respect, as it is in reproductive capacity and quality of timber, to that found in Pennsylvania. The reproduction is poor, and the tree grows very slowly both in diameter and height. The current rate of growth in diameter of 141 trees, averaging 16.6 inches in diameter, was found to average 1 inch in 25 years.

BALSAM.

Balsam is for the most part a small tree in the Adirondacks. One specimen 2 feet in diameter was measured, but the average of trees over 10 inches in diameter is between 11 and 12 inches. A very large proportion of the whole stand is under 10 inches. Balsam is most plentiful in swamps, although the largest specimens are found on the knolls above them. On wet soil it is frequently almost pure, but in such cases the trees are small.

It reproduces itself well, and the young growth bears a considerable amount of shade. The rate of growth was determined, for 63 trees averaging 10.5 inches in diameter, to be 1 inch in diameter in 13 years.

SOFT MAPLE.

The Soft Maple reaches a diameter of nearly 2 feet, and, when growing at its best, has a fair clear length. A very large proportion of the trees are unsound. In the Adirondacks Soft Maple is most abundant

in low, moist situations, but it avoids acid soil. It is found, however,
on high ground, and the largest specimens observed were on hardwood
land.

It reproduces itself well as a rule, and in some places, notably on
Spruce flats, young growth is very abundant after windfalls.

The rate of growth in diameter, for 21 trees averaging 11 inches in
diameter, was 1 inch in 17 years.

ENEMIES OF THE FOREST.

WIND.

The damage done by wind in the Adirondacks is very great. Where-
ever a second-growth forest of pure Spruce, Soft Maple, or Birch is
found a careful examination reveals traces of windfall or fire. The
Spruce is especially subject to windfall on account of its shallow root
system and its long, slender stem, which give a strong leverage to
the wind. The prevailing wind is from the southwest, and the slopes
facing this direction are most exposed to heavy storms. These slopes
are, as a rule, steep, and the soil is thin and stony; and the Spruce
which grows upon them is in consequence unable to obtain a firm foothold. It is here that the most frequent windfalls are found, and the
Spruce is often comparatively young, because the trees are blown down
before they reach maturity. (See Pl. III.)

The danger from windfall is considerable, also, on Spruce flats and
swamps where the ground is moist and the soil thin. On rolling flats
it is common to find extensive areas where the conifers have been blown
down and their place has been taken by Soft Maple and Birch. Frequently, however, the entire tract is swept clear, and either pure Spruce
or a mixture of conifers and hardwoods follow as the second growth.
The soil in these sections is usually meager and often underlaid with an
impermeable subsoil. On the knolls and ridges rising out of swamps
the trees are chiefly coniferous and are frequently blown over by the
storms. On the hardwood lands, on the other hand, where the soil is
comparatively deep and there is a large admixture of hardwoods, the
danger is small.

Hemlock is about as easily overturned by storms as Spruce, but it
usually occurs in mixture, and is therefore protected by other species.
White Pine is comparatively wind firm. The tall shafts tower many
feet above the rest of the forest and are exposed to winds from all
directions, but they are uprooted only by the heaviest storms. Of the
hardwoods, Birch is most easily overturned.

The wind injures the forest not only by uprooting trees but by actually breaking or splitting the stems. Hollow Spruces are frequently
snapped off at the butt and trees weakened with cancer or other dis-
eases are often broken at the affected spot. Balsam is very susceptible
to breakage by the wind on account of its brittle wood. Rotten trees

A BALSAM TOP BROKEN OFF BY THE WIND AND LODGED IN AN ELM. SANTA CLARA, N. Y

are readily snapped off at the butt, and often sound trees are broken down. Balsam tops heavily loaded with cones are unable to withstand heavy winds. A marked example of this is shown in Pl. XIII.

Constant racking of trees by the wind sometimes causes large seams which run through the entire stem. (See Pl. XIV, fig. 2.) It is not uncommon for such seamy trees to become twisted and broken down by strong winds. Shakes or large cracks, following the grain of the wood, are often caused at the base of large trees, especially of Pine and Hemlock.

FIRE.

Recent fires have done but little damage on the two tracts considered in this report. In fact there are but two conspicuous instances of fire burning over more than an acre or two within the last decade, and these were confined to a very limited area. Formerly the land was less carefully guarded and fire was frequently started by campers. The effects of old fires are found in abundance on sandy points on the lakes, and there are a number of steep mountains which were burned over fully 20 years ago and are now becoming restocked with timber. There are three such high ridges in the Whitney Preserve and one in Nehasane Park, on which the timber was entirely destroyed by old fires and on which the tree growth is now beginning to return.

During the greater part of the year the forest is so damp that fire will not run easily. When a fire once gains headway, however, it is extremely difficult to extinguish it, because it burns in the deep vegetable duff and smoulders for weeks and even months, defying all efforts to put it out. The damage by such a fire is very great, and usually all the timber is killed on the area burned over. Spruce and Balsam are especially subject to injury from fire.

Where the timber is destroyed on the sandy shores of lakes the return of the forest is very quick, for the surface cover is merely burned off and the deep soil remains in a receptive condition for the seed. On steep slopes, on the other hand, there is but little or no soil under the vegetable cover, and when this is burned off there is practically nothing but bare rock left to receive the seed. In such places seedlings do not return for many years. The reproduction after fire is slow also on the rolling flats where the soil is extremely thin and is covered with stones and bowlders. Pl. XIV, fig. 1, illustrates the effect of fire in such a situation.

In certain sections of the Adirondacks the destruction of the forest by fire has been very great. This is notably the case in the northwestern portion of the mountains, where considerable areas, especially near the railroad, have been burned over. After lumbering, the danger from fire is always increased, on account of the large amount of inflammable material left in the form of tops, culled logs, broken saplings, etc., and also because the leaves and other material on the ground become very dry through the thinning of the forest and admission of the sunlight and wind. This is especially true where a considerable amount of Pine occurs, for in felling the heavy trees large openings are inevitably made and the tops, saturated with pitch, are very inflammable.

INSECTS.

The Spruce forests of the Adirondacks have at different periods been attacked by what is locally known as the Spruce blight, the cause of which is now recognized to be a small bark beetle, *Dendroctonus rufipennis* Kirby. It appears that in certain sections of New York State large numbers of Spruce died between 1840 and 1850 and that there was a repetition of the same trouble about 20 years later. Between 1875 and 1880 the forests were again attacked by borers, and during the following 10 years a large amount of valuable timber was killed. The borers seem to attack sound, thrifty trees as soon as they begin to work in large numbers, but they do not, as a rule, attack trees under about 10 inches in diameter. The death of the timber is caused by the numerous galleries made by the borers between the wood and bark, which virtually girdle the trees. The forests of northern New Hampshire and Maine are said to be subject to the attacks of this insect at the present time, and it would not be surprising if there were another outbreak of the pest in the Adirondacks.

The Tamarack in the Adirondacks has suffered even more from the attacks of insects than the Spruce. In fact, practically all the large timber has either been killed or is dying from the work of the larvæ of a sawfly, *Nematus erichsoni* Hartig, which entirely defoliate the trees. This pest made its appearance about 1882 and still continues its destructive work. It is now difficult to find living specimens of Tamarack over 10 inches in diameter, and a large number of the small trees show some injurious effects from the worm. (See Pl. VII, fig. 2.)

WATER.

It is well known that the flooding of the shores of streams and lakes during the season of vegetation destroys the timber. About bodies of water where the surface level has been raised by dams built for logging purposes there is usually a fringe of dead timber. Where, however, the water is raised only in the early spring and let out immediately after the logs have been driven, the damage is very small. When the water is raised above its normal level by dams in the early winter there is frequently a certain amount of damage by the washing of the shores during heavy winds. (Pl. XV, figs. 1 and 2.)

ICE.

While the injury caused by the submerging of the roots during the season of vegetation is well known, the damage resulting from high water in winter has not been generally recognized. The reason for this

FIG. 1.—EFFECTS OF A FOREST FIRE. BIG BROOK, WHITNEY PRESERVE.

FIG. 2.—A SPRUCE WITH A LARGE SEAM, CAUSED PROBABLY BY THE WIND.
WHITNEY PRESERVE.

is that in the majority of cases, where timber has been killed by flooding, the water was held up during a part or the whole of the summer months and the exact proportion of the damage done during the winter can not be determined. The writer has been fortunate in finding a single case where the water in a small pond was raised about 2 feet in the autumn and lowered in May, and, as a result of the flooding, the trees whose roots were submerged were killed.

Bum Pond, where the flooding occurred, is situated in township 36, Hamilton County, N. Y. It is about a quarter of a mile long and about 100 yards wide, with comparatively low shores surrounded by Spruce, second-growth Pine, Tamarack, Balsam, and a few Yellow Birch. According to the statement of Mr. Ernest H. Johnson, of Little Tupper Lake, New York, who built the dam, all the trees, including the Tamaracks, were alive before the water was raised. The next season the foliage of the trees which had stood in the water became red, and all died before winter. The following statement of Mr. Johnson will show exactly when he built the dam, when the water was lowered, and what injury was done to the timber according to his observation:

LITTLE TUPPER LAKE, *December 2, 1893.*

In November, the fall of 1893, I built a small dam for Dr. A. L. Loomis on the outlet of Bum Pond, in township 36, Hamilton County, N. Y., and raised the water about 2 feet. Early in May the dam broke through and the water drained down to its former level. The dam was not filled again that summer, but the trees that had stood in the water and had been frozen in the ice all died during the summer, which was the result (I should say) of being frozen in and girdled by the ice, as the bark, just at the high-water line, all peeled off.

ERNEST H. JOHNSON.

There can be no doubt that the trees were girdled by the ice. On many of the small trees with thin bark the latter had been cut and had peeled off exactly at the high-water line. The trees with thick bark had been killed, but the bark had, in most cases, remained intact. It would appear that the girdling was done by the action of the ice, frozen about the trees, when the level of the water was changed. The strain upon the trees must be very great when the water is raised, and the weight of the ice must tend to force the bark from the tree when the water falls. The full physiological explanation of the phenomenon must, however, be left for further study.

The effect of winter flooding at Bum Pond is shown in Pl. XVI, figs. 1 and 2.

LOSSES THROUGH ORDINARY LUMBERING.

There is an increasing tendency among the lumbermen in the Adirondacks to avoid unnecessary waste in lumbering. Many companies are doing excellent work in this regard, but with the majority there still remains considerable room for improvement, especially where the lumbering is done under the system of contracts and subcontracts. The temptation for a jobber to do careless work is very great. Unless carefully watched he is apt to cut unnecessarily high stumps, to leave large tops in order to avoid the trouble of trimming off the branches, to leave trees lodged in hardwoods, and otherwise to fall below the standard of good lumbering. (Pl. XVII, fig. 2.)

The principal loss arising from careless lumbering is occasioned by—

(1) Needlessly high stumps.
(2) Large tops.
(3) Skids left in the woods.
(4) Valuable timber used in leveling roads.
(5) Destruction of small growth in felling, skidding, and hauling.

LOSS BY CUTTING HIGH STUMPS.

When the trees are felled by chopping. the stumps are cut at the point at which the axe naturally falls when the chopper stands erect. This is usually about 3 feet above the ground. The majority of trees, however, are sawed down, and their stumps are somewhat lower. averaging about 30 inches in height. (Pl. XVII, fig. 1; Pl. XX, fig. 1.) The sawyers protest against cutting low stumps, because it tires their backs to stoop over, and in order to avoid trouble with the men the foreman usually allows them to do as they please in the matter. Experience by careful lumbermen has proved that such high stumps are entirely needless. In the following table the average height of stumps of trees 9, 10, 11, and 12 inches in diameter. cut in Nehasane in 1897, is compared to that of trees cut in Franklin County by the Santa Clara Lumber Company in 1896, where a special effort was made to cut stumps as low as possible. No figures are given for trees over 12 inches through, because the Santa Clara Lumber Company was lumbering on cut-over land and there were but few trees above this size

Average height of stumps cut at Santa Clara, N. Y., in 1896, and at Nehasane, N. Y., in 1897.

Diameter of trees.	Average height of stumps.	
	Santa Clara.	Nehasane.
Inches.	Inches.	Inches.
9	17	26
10	16	25
11	19	26
12	20	29

In the Adirondacks the timber is scaled by measuring the logs at the small end after they have been placed on the skidway. The measurements are always taken in even inches. Thus. a log 6.3 inches in

FIG. 1.—WASHING OF THE SHORE OF LITTLE TUPPER LAKE BY HIGH WATER, CAUSED BY AN UNNECESSARILY HIGH DAM.

FIG. 2.—INJURY TO THE SHORE OF LITTLE TUPPER LAKE BY HIGH WATER.

diameter is called even 6, and 7.8 even 8, etc. If a lower stump is cut the top of each log is lower on the tree and is therefore larger in diameter. Where the measurement of a log is near the dividing line between two whole inches this increase would in many cases be sufficient to make it scale 1 inch larger than it would where a high stump is cut. Thus, a log measuring 6.4 inches in diameter would probably scale 0.3 inch more if the stump were cut a foot lower, in which case the scalers would call it a 7-inch instead of a 6-inch log.

In order to compute the loss occasioned by cutting high stumps, the following method was used: Two hundred and eighty-three trees, which were measured in Nehasane Park in 1897, were scaled in standards. The taper of each log in each tree was computed, and it was determined what the diameter at the top of each would have been if the stump had been cut 18 inches above the ground.

It was found that out of these 283 trees 78 would have actually scaled more in standards if low stumps had been cut. Computation was made of the percentage of increase in each tree affected and of the ratio of trees of each diameter, showing an increase to the entire number measured.

In the table on page 60 it will be seen that the trees of small diameter show the greatest percentage of increase in standards, and that those of large diameter show the greatest percentage of individuals affected.

The total increase for all the trees amounted to 5.4 standards. The total yield of the trees was 258 standards. The percentage of increase was therefore 2.1. The trees from which this computation was made were all sound. In actual practice a number of the trees are found to have some imperfection at the stump and a short piece has to be cut off. In generalizing from the above figures, therefore, an allowance should be made for trees of this character. It is believed that a reduction of 5 per cent is ample. The figure 2.1 per cent should be, therefore, 2 per cent.

These figures mean that for every 100,000 standards removed 2,000 are wasted by cutting high stumps. If a tract of 100,000 acres yields on an average 15 standards per acre, there would be a loss in cutting high stumps of 30,000 standards. At a stumpage value of 40 cents per standard, this represents an actual loss of $12,000.

Number and percentage of trees, showing increased scale by cutting low stumps and percentage of increase in standards of those trees.

Diameter, breast high.	Trees measured.	Trees showing increased scale on account of low stumps.		Increase in standards.
Inches.	Number.	Number.	Per cent.	Per cent.
9	17	2	12	16
10	37	1	3	16
11	46	9	20	12
12	27	7	25	11
13	28	10	35	9
14	39	11	28	7
15	16	2	12	5
16	11	6	50	7
17	12	3	25	6
18	17	9	50	6
19	10	6	60	7
20	5	3	60	1
21	3	1	30	5
22	5	2	40	7
23	5	4	80	3
24	5	2	40	2
Total	283	78	....	....

LOSS BY LEAVING LARGE TOPS IN THE WOODS.

Where lumbering is done under contract it has been the usual custom in the Adirondacks to cut only logs which will scale 6 inches at the top end. Where timber is cut for pulp, smaller logs can be used, and many companies which operate their own camps compel the choppers to cut logs as small as 5 and often 4 inches. In the vicinity of Nehasane Park it has been the custom to cut no logs under 6 inches in diameter, but in actual practice the average size of the top log is nearer 8 inches. There are thus, in the majority of cases, 4 to 12 feet of wood left in most tops, which is fit for pulp and which is actually so used by many companies. (Pl. XVIII. fig. 1.)

The point will at once be raised that the tops are knotty and the wood of an inferior quality. The reply is that many companies use this material, and that the total amount is so great that it would pay to utilize it, even if it were possible to sell it for only one-fourth the price of the rest of the timber.

The 283 trees already mentioned as having been scaled in Nehasane Park were used as the basis of the computation of the amount wasted in this way. From measurements taken in the top it was possible to determine how many 4-foot billets over 5 inches in diameter could be cut from each. The exact cubic contents of these billets which could have been cut was then determined. It was found that this material amounted to 6.3 per cent of the total contents of the trees actually used. Inasmuch as this portion of the tree is inferior to the rest of the

FIG. 1.—YOUNG TREES KILLED BY WINTER FLOODING: BUM POND, WHITNEY PRESERVE.
The trees appear to have been girdled by the ice.

FIG. 2.—A YOUNG WHITE PINE KILLED BY WINTER FLOODING: WHITNEY PRESERVE.

wood it is fair to reckon that a stumpage price of only 10 cents per standard could be obtained, as against 30 to 40 cents, the value of average Spruce timber. If the total yield were 15 standards per acre, an increase of 6.5 per cent would be 0.95 standard per acre. At 10 cents per standard this would amount to 9.5 cents per acre, or on 1,000 acres to $95.

If this material were used there would be not only a substantial profit but in order to get it out it would be necessary to lop so many of the branches that no further trimming would be necessary as a precaution against the spread of fire.

LOSS IN BUILDING SKIDWAYS.

The majority of skidways are built of Spruce. The tree has a long, clean, straight stem, is quickly cut down, and easily handled. Moreover, the bark is rough and holds the logs from slipping. Hardwoods, on the other hand, are heavy to handle, require a longer time to cut than Spruce, and even when straight are often covered with burls and other irregularities which make it difficult to roll logs over them. Sometimes Hemlock and, in swamps, Balsam are used for the main skids. The lumbermen object to Balsam, however, on the ground that the average trees are not strong enough for the large skidways, and that the bark is too slippery to hold the logs.

It is desirable, when possible, to use other material than Spruce and Pine for skids and all other lumbering purposes, because the presence of small specimens of these trees, which will grow to merchantable size in a comparatively short time, tends to enhance the value of lumbered land much more than the same amount of young growth of other species. Smaller trees are merchantable in the case of Spruce than of any other species, which fact, coupled with its rapid growth on cut-over land, makes it possible to obtain repeated crops at shorter intervals. As yet the small hardwoods have but little recognized importance in the market for future growth, and the loss of the few trees which would be cut for lumbering purposes would not be felt.

It should be said in this connection that the use of a certain amount of Spruce for skids in the first cutting may not seriously affect the forest to its injury, but if the hardwoods and Hemlocks are cut within a few years a similar thinning of the Spruce for lumbering purposes would impair the future value of the forest.

For the construction of each skidway at least three trees are necessary, but for those which hold 200 to 300 logs from four to six trees are often used. Since a certain number of the skids are from hardwood trees, Hemlock, and Balsam, it is estimated that not more than three Spruce trees are cut for the average skidway. A careful study has shown that an average skidway holds the product of about 3 acres, so that the use of Spruce for skids amounts to about one tree per acre. It is estimated that these trees yield, on an average, one-fourth standard each, or on 1,000 acres, 250 standards. At 40 cents per standard the stumpage value of the timber would amount to $100. It is the custom at present to leave the skids in the woods (Pl. XIX, figs. 1 and 2), in which case the owner loses not only the stumpage value of the timber thus wasted, but also the advantage of future increment which the trees would take on, if left standing. It is estimated from figures obtained in connection with the study of the Spruce mentioned on page 40 that these trees would in 25 years grow 4 inches in diameter. The trees yield at the present about one-fourth standard each, but, if left standing 25 years, would yield not less than 0.6 standard each; 1,000 trees would then yield at the end of 25 years 600 standards. By cutting them now for lumbering purposes and leaving them in the woods, the owner is losing not only the present value of the trees, but also the increment, which in 25 years would amount to 350 standards—the difference between the present yield, 250 standards, and 600 standards, the yield in 25 years.

LOSS IN BUILDING ROADS.

There has been a prevailing impression among lumbermen that the foresters propose to lay out roads themselves. A good lumberman can lay out his roads as well as a forester, and better in most cases, because he has had more experience in the particular locality in question. But all the contractors and foremen are not good lumbermen, and the laying out of the roads varies considerably in different lumber jobs. It is of advantage to the contractor to have his roads few and short, because he has to pay the cost of cutting them and breaking them out in winter. The owner benefits by having as few roads as possible, because each one means so much cleared land and so much timber cut down, which in the case of valuable hardwoods is wasted. Some contractors cut up the woods with many more roads than are necessary, thereby shortening the distance for skidding logs, but making necessary a large number of small instead of a small number of large skidways. The larger the number of roads the greater the number of seed trees which are cut down, and the larger the number of skidways the greater the number of trees needed for skids. A considerable amount of small timber is always used to level the roads, build bridges, etc. (Pl. XVIII, fig. 2). Spruce is the easiest timber to handle and is always attacked for this purpose, except in swamps, where there is usually an abundance of Balsam near at hand. As a result, the lumbermen cut many seed trees and much young growing timber where crooked and unsound hardwoods would answer the purpose equally well. It is impossible to draw a sharp line and absolutely prevent the use of Spruce for roads, for, occasionally, it is not practicable to use anything else. But in most cases it is entirely feasible to use some other material. The experiment of compelling the contractor to use hardwoods for leveling roads has been tried with entire success in New Hampshire, where it is much less plentiful than in the Adirondacks.

FIG. 1.—WASTE IN LUMBERING: A SPRUCE STUMP CUT 18 INCHES TOO HIGH. WHITNEY PRESERVE.

FIG 2.—WASTE IN LUMBERING: A SOUND SPRUCE YIELDING TWO LOGS LEFT LODGED IN THE WOODS. WHITNEY PRESERVE.

The actual loss caused by the use of Spruce in building roads can not be estimated accurately, because the trees used are generally small, and no market value can be placed upon many of them. But as a basis for the future crops they have sufficient value to prohibit their removal except where really necessary.

LOSS TO YOUNG GROWTH IN FELLING.

Reference has already been made to the large amount of young Spruce throughout the forest. (Pl. I.) This young growth is to form the main part of the crops to be cut during the next 50 years, and it is extremely desirable that as little be destroyed as possible. There is usually more than one direction in which a tree can be thrown by means of wedges, and it is perfectly possible to do the felling with very little injury to the small growth without additional expense. Many sawyers take pride in felling the trees without making a slash, and in such cases but little young growth is damaged. Fully 50 per cent of the sawyers, however, cut the trees in a most careless manner and take no pains whatever in regard to smashing young timber. The careless sawyers should be made to do as good work as those who are careful of their own accord.

INJURY DONE IN SKIDDING.

As a rule, the logs cut upon about 3 acres are rolled on one skidway. It is thus necessary to drag the logs a considerable distance through the woods. A large number of small trees are broken in this way, and foresters who are not in full touch with the conditions of this country often feel that a large amount of unnecessary damage is being done. As a matter of fact, there is usually only one path by which it is practical to "snake" a log from the stump to the skidway. Anyone who observes a gutterman at work will see at once that he picks out the path where there are the fewest obstructions, like fallen logs, stumps, and brush. Everything in this path must be cleared, exactly as all trees and brush must be cut away in building a lumber road; and the loss of small trees caused by the trailing of logs must be considered in exactly the same light as that caused by building roads. If a careful examination is made of the forest growth after skidding it will be found that the total loss caused in this way is in the aggregate insignificant. The contractor should, however, be made to use every precaution to do no unnecessary damage to the young growth.

DESTRUCTION OF SMALL GROWTH IN HAULING.

This takes place on steep roads, where the men frequently scatter Spruce brush to check the speed of the sleds. It often happens that all the young Spruce left standing by the choppers near such steep roads are cut to supply the brush for this purpose, and the stems are left lying on the ground to decay. (Pl. XX, fig 2.) Careful lumber-men use marsh hay or manure to stop the sleds on steep inclines, and the slashing of small Spruce for this purpose is considered wasteful and unnecessary.

SPECIAL WORKING PLAN FOR THE TWO TRACTS.

DIAMETER LIMIT FOR CUTTING SPRUCE.

Where a company is operating its own camps in the Adirondacks, Spruce logs are usually cut for pulp as small as 5 inches in diameter at the small end, and there are almost no sound trees left standing over 6 inches in diameter on the stump. On the other hand, where the logs are cut under contract, it is usually customary to use only such as will square 6 inches, and the timber is cut to about 8 inches on the stump. In the first case it is estimated that it will be fully 75 years before a second crop equal to the first can be obtained, and if the timber is cut to 8 inches, 50 years will be required. Under this system of cutting a third crop would require even a longer period for growth than the second, because most of the trees capable of bearing seed would have been removed, and much of the ground which might have come up to Spruce, had there been a sufficient number of trees to dis-tribute seed, would be covered with hardwoods.

Whether it is best to restrict the cutting of Spruce in the Adirondacks to 10, 12, or 14 inches in diameter depends upon a variety of circum-stances. In certain sections it may be best to leave the majority of trees under 14 inches, in other sections only those under 10 inches, and in some few localities everything ought to be removed on account of the danger from windfall. In most places on the western side of the Adirondacks it will be safe to cut the Spruce as low as 10 inches, pro-vided a sufficient number of the seed trees are left standing. There are, on an average, 40 to 50 trees per acre between 5 and 10 inches in diameter, of which about 50 per cent bear a certain amount of seed. This number, supplemented by larger trees when necessary, is probably sufficient to maintain the present proportion of Spruce in the forest for succeeding generations. Much better results as regards reproduction would, however, be obtained if all trees under 12 inches in diameter were left standing, for then there would be a larger number of seed trees. Moreover, those 10 and 11 inches in diameter bear more abun-dantly than the smaller ones. If 12 inches were made the minimum limit of cutting, a second crop could be obtained in a shorter period and the annual growth of merchantable timber would be greater than if the trees were cut as small as 10 inches. From Table A, page 47, it will be seen that a forest which has a yield of about 3,000 board feet per acre will produce the same amount again 36 years after the first cutting, if all trees 10 inches and over in diameter are left standing.

FIG. 1.—WASTE IN LUMBERING : A TOP LEFT BY LUMBERMEN FROM WHICH A MERCHANTABLE LOG COULD HAVE BEEN CUT. WHITNEY PRESERVE.

FIG. 2.—SMALL SPRUCE USED IN LEVELING A LUMBER ROAD. WHITNEY PRESERVE.

If, on the other hand, 12 inches is made the minimum limit for cutting, the first cut will be 2,490 board feet, which amount can again be obtained in 24 years. (See Table B, page 48.) In the first case the growth of merchantable timber is 83 board feet, in the second 104 board feet per acre per annum. The land will, therefore, produce more timber in the long run if the trees under 12 inches in diameter are left standing than if only those under 10 inches remain. In the case of Nehasane Park and the Whitney Preserve, however, the owners wish to obtain the greatest possible immediate return without seriously impairing the productive power of the forest, and are willing to wait a longer period for a second cut. It is recommended, therefore, that 10 inches be made the minimum limit for cutting Spruce. The prediction of the future yield on the two tracts can be made by reference to the yield tables on pages 47 and 48, as is shown in the following paragraphs:

PREDICTION OF FUTURE YIELD IN NEHASANE PARK.

On page 74 the exact amount of Spruce cut during the season 1898–99 is shown to be 13.15 standards per acre, or 2,630 board feet per acre, if one standard log contains 200 board feet, as is usually estimated in the Adirondacks. This yield is smaller than the estimate given for the average stand per acre over the whole park in "The Adirondack Spruce." The small yield is explained by the fact that a larger proportion of swamp land occurs on the section cut over than elsewhere; that a wide strip along the railroad had been cut over for ties; that there is a large windfall area on which no merchantable timber at all stood; that a considerable number of trees were left for seed, because they contained only one log or were not readily accessible, and that the lumbermen wasted a certain amount of Spruce in building skidways. In the portion of the park lumbered during the past season 217 acres were surveyed by the writer in 1897 and found to average 2,584 board feet per acre, or slightly below the actual amount cut.

In view of the fact that there is a large amount of promising young Spruce on the windfall area, as well as on the tract lumbered for ties, and that many patches of trees and individuals in swamps and inaccessible places were left standing by the lumbermen, it is fair to base the computation of future yield on a present stand of at least 3,000 board feet per acre.

Inasmuch as the timber is cut to a minimum limit of 10 inches, Table A, page 47, should be used in the calculation of future crops. On areas with an average stand of 3,000 board feet there can be cut in 10 years 11 per cent of the original stand, or 330 board feet; in 20 years, 41 per per cent, or 1,230 board feet; in 30 years, 70 per cent, or 2,100 board feet; and the original amount—namely, 3,000 board feet—can be obtained in 36 years.

PREDICTION OF FUTURE YIELD IN THE WHITNEY PRESERVE.

The actual amount of timber cut during the past season was 14.6 standards per acre, or 2,920 board feet, considering 1 standard equivalent to 200 board feet (see page 76). This amount is so near 3,000 board feet that the computation of future yield in Nehasane Park, as given above, may be used also for the Whitney Preserve, namely, that the original cut can be obtained in 36 years, and that 330, 1,230, and 2,100 board feet per acre can be obtained in 10, 20, and 30 years, respectively.

IMPORTANCE OF SAVING THE SMALL SPRUCE.

There is throughout the forest a large amount of small Spruce not yet of merchantable size, which, if left standing, will in a comparatively short time be suitable for pulp and lumber. Until recently this small material has not been recognized as having any particular value and no attempt has been made to protect it. Many small trees have, however, been left standing because they could not be sold or because they were not needed for skids, road building, etc., and in many instances lumbermen who have cut over their land a second time have secured crops almost, if not quite, equal to that obtained at the first cutting. As a result they are beginning to appreciate the importance of sparing the small trees, in order that a second cut may be obtained sooner than would otherwise be possible; and there is a general tendency throughout the Adirondacks to limit the cutting of Spruce to 10 or 12 inches on the stump. Hitherto the presence of a large amount of young growth in the forest has not materially influenced the sale value of land in the Adirondacks, but it may be confidently expected that there will be a demand for such land by large paper companies, just as is already the case in New Hampshire, where land stocked with small trees has actually been sold for a high price in view of its future value.

PREVIOUS ATTEMPTS AT CONSERVATIVE LUMBERING.

A number of efforts have been made in the Adirondacks to lumber Spruce on conservative principles. The plan usually adopted is to remove all trees measuring 10 inches and over on the stump. This system is a long step in advance of cutting to 6 or 8 inches, but it has two serious defects: First, the measurement of the trees is left entirely to the choppers; second, no provision is made to leave seed trees in places where there are not enough small Spruce capable of bearing fruit to answer the purpose.

NEED OF MARKING THE TIMBER.

In the actual practice of the system described in the previous section the lumbermen cut to less than 10 inches in diameter on the stump. In fact, there is hardly an attempt to even estimate the diameter. The sawyers are instructed to cut all trees yielding two 14-foot logs which will scale not less than 6 inches at the top end, inside the bark. The majority of such trees are above 10 inches in diameter at the stump, but not all. Thus, out of about 300 trees measured in Nehasane Park, where the lumbermen endeavored in 1897 to restrict the cutting to 10 inches, over 2 per cent were under 10 inches on the stump. In order to be certain that no trees are cut under 10 inches in diameter, and to show the sawyers what trees should be left standing for seeding purposes, it is necessary to mark those which are to be cut.

NECESSITY OF LEAVING SEED TREES.

If the trees under 10 inches in diameter, capable of bearing seed, were evenly distributed over the area, they would be entirely sufficient to bring about the desired reproduction of Spruce in the openings made in lumbering; but there are many places where seed trees under 10 inches are entirely absent, and where one or two Spruce above this size ought to be left standing to insure an ample reproduction. (Pl. II, fig. 1.) These places are especially abundant on hardwood land and Spruce flats, where the reproduction of Spruce finds considerable difficulty in competition with other species. Here it is often necessary to leave on an average 4 to 6 trees per acre over 10 inches in diameter for seeding purposes. In swamps, on the other hand, the number of seed trees required over 10 inches in diameter is not large. This is explained by the fact that in the swamps the trees are of comparatively even age and seed early in life, and in consequence there are a large number of small trees capable of bearing fruit. On Spruce slopes also the number of trees needed for seed is small, because there are frequent groups of trees about 6 to 10 inches in diameter which distribute a large amount of seed and because the conditions of reproduction are so favorable to the Spruce that a considerable amount of small seedlings growth is already to be found.

RULES FOR CUTTING SPRUCE.

The general principles governing the selection of timber for removal are—

(1) To remove all trees measuring 10 inches and over in diameter at 3 feet from the ground, except those needed for seed.

(2) To remove all trees under 10 inches in diameter which will probably not live till the second cutting and which may be profitably cut now.

RULES FOR MARKING TIMBER.

The following rules should be observed in marking the timber:

(1) All tall trees 15 inches and over in diameter should be marked for removal. On page 33 it is shown that the large trees are very old,

those 15 inches in diameter averaging over 200 years. Although a large number of these are growing rapidly and may live many years, they have reached merchantable size and in many instances are beginning to show signs of decline. This old timber should be removed before it decays, or is injured by insects. wind, or otherwise. A place is seldom found where it would pay to leave a Spruce 15 inches in diameter for seed, for either there are enough smaller trees at hand to answer the purpose, or the conditions for reproduction are so unfavorable that the results obtained by leaving a mature tree, worth fully 30 cents on the stump, would not justify the investment. The exception to the rule is where a short, scrubby tree, 15 inches or over in diameter, which contains only a small amount of coarse timber, would serve as a good seed tree.

(2) All very old trees which are under 15 inches in diameter, and which may die before the end of the probable interval between the first and second cuts, should be marked for removal. The old timber may be easily distinguished from the young at a glance. The most obvious sign is the diameter and height; but where trees are about the same size, other signs must be used. A tree which carries its diameter well up into the crown is usually pretty old, while a tapering stem and slender top are signs of youth. A young tree often has a low. conical crown, with a long, slender head. Old trees, on the other hand, are charac terized by thick, blunt crowns. The general age can often be detected by the color of the bark. When the upper part of the stem is reddish and has a comparatively smooth bark roughened by delicate scales, the tree is young. When the bark in the crown is thick and has heavy, gray scales, the tree is old.

(3) All trees which show signs of decay, but which are still mer chantable, should be marked for removal. The most obvious sign of decay in Spruce is the exudation of resin on the stem. The presence of hardened gum on old branch wounds is not necessarily a sign of internal decay, but soft, white resin is a sure indication that the tree is unsound, at least where the resin comes out. It frequently happens that, while gum is found on the lower part of the tree, the upper por tion of the stem is perfectly sound. Thus the lumbermen usually cut a large tree, even if "gummy," with the hope of finding one or two sound logs in the upper part of the stem. A small tree which shows this sign is usually useless. The presence of "punk knots" is a sure test of unsoundness. These are found at points where branches have been broken off. and usually manifest themselves by a slight bulge. and if cut, are found to be rotten. Sometimes on old trees these punk knots are difficult to distinguish. The disease is especially common on Pines. and is known as "blind punk." An experienced woodsman can distinguish an unsound tree by striking it with an ax. A sound tree has a peculiar ring, which to a trained ear readily distinguishes it from the dull or hollow sound of a rotten trunk. The appearance of the bark and foliage is often a test of the health of the tree. A

healthy tree usually has scaly, rough bark; a dying tree, soft, smooth bark. If it is found to be dry and to peel with difficulty in the spring, it is also a sign that the tree is dying. The foliage of a sickly tree is frequently thin, straggling, and dark colored. If the top is dry or there are dead branches covered with moss within the crown, the tree is apt to be unsound. A tree with a large seam is not necessarily unsound. The seam unfits it for lumber, but not for pulp.

(4) All merchantable trees which are likely to be blown down should be marked for removal.

(5) All merchantable trees which have been partially girdled by porcupines or rubbing of other trees should be marked for removal. There are considerable numbers of such trees which are perfectly sound, but which have been partially girdled in the crown and will decay or actually die during a period of 25 or 30 years.

RULES FOR SELECTING SEED TREES.

Seed trees are left for two purposes: First, to supply a basis for future growth; second, to seed the ground to Spruce. The first of these objects is accomplished by leaving all trees under 10 inches in diameter. The second is secured partly by the trees under 10 inches in diameter and partly by larger specimens left especially for that purpose. The choice of the latter requires great care and judgment.

(1) The smallest tree available for the purpose should be selected.

(2) When possible, only trees with less than three 14-foot logs should be selected.

(3) Those with the quickest taper—that is, the youngest trees—should always be chosen. It has been shown on page 68 that a quick taper is usually a sign of youth and vigor.

(4) Only such trees as have their crowns exposed to light from above should be chosen, for light is necessary for the production of seed, and the seed trees must be capable of bearing fruit at once or within a short period.

(5) Only sound, vigorous specimens should be selected.

(6) Unsound trees which can not be utilized should always be left standing. If felled, as is required by many lumbermen, the trees are left in the woods, making food for fire. If left standing, they distribute a certain amount of seed.

(7) All trees whose branches are locked in valuable hardwoods and which can not be removed without cutting the latter should be left standing. The hardwoods will probably be marketable in a few years and the Spruce can be taken out at that time.

(8) Where an opening is to be made in lumbering one or more seed trees should be located on the side toward the prevailing wind, so that the seed will be blown over the ground.

(9) On a slope the seed trees should be located above rather than below a large opening.

(10) A tree should never be left for seed which will be struck or injured by the felling of others. In almost every case a good seed tree can be found which is protected from the lumbering by some hardwood or Hemlock.

(11) A seed tree should not be located where the ground is already well seeded with Spruce or other species, or where there are other trees which will answer the purpose equally well.

RULES FOR THE LUMBERMEN.

(1) No trees should be cut which are not marked, unless a satisfactory reason can be given for so doing.

(2) All marked trees should be cut, unless a satisfactory reason can be given for not doing so.

(3) No Spruce should be used in building bridges, corduroy, skids, or for any other lumbering purposes, unless it is impracticable to use other material.

The above rules were adopted for the first year's lumbering. In the plan for the second year's work they were amplified, and are given in full on pages 76 and 77.

PLAN FOR CUTTING WHITE PINE AND OTHER SPECIES.

Practically all of the merchantable Pine on the two tracts has reached maturity and a very large amount of it is affected with decay and wind shake. It should, therefore, be removed as rapidly as possible, and there should be no restrictions in regard to the size of timber to be cut. There should also be no restrictions in cutting the merchantable Cherry and Balsam, as they are very scattered and their removal will not injure the forest. The present condition of the market makes it unwise to cut Hemlock and the hardwoods during the present season.

THE FIRST YEAR'S WORK.

NEHASANE PARK.

The working plan just described was put into execution in 1898 on the two tracts under consideration. In Nehasane Park the stumpage of the Spruce, Pine, and a small amount of Balsam and Cherry was sold to the contracting parties who carried on the lumbering. Four camps were operated, two by the contractor and two by subcontractors. The total amount of timber cut is given on page 74.

In accordance with an arrangement with the owner of the park, as described in the introduction, the Division of Forestry superintended the work of marking the timber which was to be cut, and inspected the land from time to time to see that the lumbering was done satisfactorily. The results of the first year's work are here discussed.

MARKING.

The work of marking timber in Nehasane Park was begun August 6, 1898, and was completed during the first week in November. During most of this time three men were employed to mark the trees, but the force was increased to four during part of the time. The writer superintended the marking, and at first designated all trees which were to be marked until the assistants were thoroughly familiar with the system of selecting the trees and were able to work independently.

The method of marking trees which was finally adopted was to blaze the butt of every Spruce below the stump with a special marking hatchet and to stamp the spot with the hatchet head, on which the initials "U. S." were cut. The choppers were instructed not to fell any trees which were not marked. The blazes on the stump made it possible to determine afterwards whether their instructions were carried out. On one lumber job the following method of marking was tried at first: The trees selected for seed, over 10 inches in diameter, were marked with one blaze, and those selected to be removed were marked with two blazes. The choppers were instructed to cut no trees as large as 10 inches in diameter on the stump except those marked with two blazes, and to cut no trees over 10 inches except those marked with one blaze. This method was very rapid and inexpensive, and was tried on a small area to test its practicability. The choppers were, however, utterly unable to determine the size of the trees, and merely cut every individual which would make two logs over 6 inches in diameter. Another experiment was tried at Forked Lake, in the Whitney Preserve, of marking only the trees between 10 and 14 inches. The sawyers were then instructed to cut all very large trees, but no small ones unless marked. This proved a failure, because it took just as long to mark the timber in this way as to blaze every tree, on account of the greater difficulty under the former method in keeping track of those which had been marked. It was proved conclusively that the only satisfactory method was to mark every tree which was to be cut.

The most rapid work can be done by a crew of three men. They move through the woods abreast, keeping about 50 feet apart and marking every tree between them, each watching the man at his side to see that no trees are missed. The inside man follows the previous line of marks and the others are guided by him. The outside man spots a hardwood tree occasionally where the Spruce are not abundant enough to have the marks serve as a line. On an average a crew of three men can mark about 40 to 60 acres per day.

The area lumbered over was determined by the surveyors to be 4,331 acres. The timber on this entire area was marked and as nearly as could be determined on about 200 acres in addition which were not cut over.

The total cost of marking, covering the board and pay of the men and the expenses of the writer, was $513.79, which for the 4,500 acres amounted to about 12 cents per acre.

Upon the entire tract of 4,500 acres on which the timber was marked there were left 9,635 trees 10 inches and over in diameter, or slightly over 2 trees per acre. It is estimated that these trees averaged about one-fourth of one standard each. There were thus designated to be left on the whole lumbered area 2,409 standards for the purpose of seed. Of trees under 10 inches in diameter 351 were marked to be cut.

WORK OF THE CONTRACTORS.

When the work was first begun considerable difficulty was found in teaching the sawyers to cut only such trees as were marked. They had been so accustomed to remove every tree of merchantable size and character that it was some time before they could be brought to do satisfactory work. It was deemed best by the manager of Nehasane Park and the writer not to impose a penalty on the contractors the first year for occasional mistakes made by the sawyers. A considerable number of such mistakes were made by the sawyers, but in view of the fact that the work was new to the lumbermen and that no penalties were inflicted the results were very satisfactory, so far as the cutting of timber for logs was concerned. The cutting of Spruce for skids and for leveling roads, on the other hand, was more difficult to regulate, and in many places trees which had been left for seed were used for skids, and small growth was used for bridges, road bedding, etc. (Pl. XIX.)

This possible loss was, however, taken into consideration in the marking, and there were left in nearly every case other seed trees which may distribute seed over the opening made in lumbering. Much more Spruce was cut in this way than was necessary, and it is recommended in the plan for the second year that a system be adopted to prevent the cutting of trees that are not marked and using small Spruce for lumbering purposes when it can be avoided.

The best work was done on the two jobs operated by the contractor. The lumber jobs which were sublet were less satisfactory. There was less disposition to carry out the orders regarding the marking, and the lumbering itself was less intelligently carried on. The trees were carelessly felled in many cases, destroying much more young growth than was necessary; the skidding was less carefully done, and the roads were not laid out with the care and skill which ought to characterize all lumbering to-day. On all the jobs the stumps were cut unnecessarily high, a considerable number of trees were left lodged in hardwoods, and a very large number of Spruce skids were left in the woods which might have been utilized for pulp. The needless waste of small Spruce in leveling roads was particularly to be regretted. In the majority of cases there is plenty of Balsam, Hemlock, or hardwood which would answer the purpose equally well, and the use of small Spruce for this purpose is entirely unjustifiable. In a number of instances a considerable amount of small Spruce was cut by the teamsters in order to obtain brush to check the sleds on steep slopes. Such work is entirely unnecessary.

FIG. 1.—SPRUCE USED IN BUILDING A SKIDWAY AND LEFT IN THE WOODS. WHITNEY PRESERVE.

FIG. 2.—SPRUCE SKIDS LEFT IN THE WOODS. WHITNEY PRESERVE.

In spite of the unsatisfactory work of the contractor in the respects discussed, the forest is in good condition from the forester's point of view. Back from the main lumber roads this is especially true, and the object of forest management has been accomplished, for a large amount of small Spruce has been left to grow to large timber, and there are a sufficient number of seed trees well distributed over the area. By the system of inspection recommended in this report the excellent condition of the forest back from the roads should be represented throughout the entire area lumbered during the second year's work.

LOPPING OF TOPS.

In Nehasane Park the choppers were obliged in every case to lop the branches of the Spruce. The object was partly to lessen the danger from fire, and partly to facilitate hunting. Spruce tops absorb moisture very quickly if near the ground. If they are cut from the trees and strewn about the ground they decay in a short time and the danger from fire is much reduced, but if they are left propped above the ground by the branches they become exceedingly dry and increase the danger from fire. The owner wished to have the forest left in such a condition that in passing along the lumber roads and trails a hunter could have an unobstructed view through the woods. In these places, therefore, all the branches were cut, so that the stems came in contact with the ground. Within the forest, away from the trails, only the uppermost branches were cut. It was believed that this latter measure would be sufficient to prevent the danger from fire, but experience has led the writer to the conviction that the precaution can do but little good unless the branches are cut on all sides of the tree. Lopping the top branches costs 1½ cents per standard, and it is probable that the careful trimming of the branches all about the tree would cost fully 3 cents. There is a tendency on the part of the choppers to leave the work carelessly done, but 3 cents per standard should fully compensate for thorough work, and contractors ought to be held responsible if the trees are not satisfactorily lopped.

Where land yields on an average about 15 standards per acre thorough lopping would amount to 45 cents per acre. While there can be no doubt that lopping the tops materially lessens the danger from fire, the results obtained are not sufficient to justify the investment of this amount, especially when the land is carefully watched, as at Nehasane Park. The writer has therefore recommended for the second year that the branches be not lopped except for sporting purposes.

EFFECT OF LUMBERING ON REPRODUCTION.

Reference has been made to the unusual amount of seed produced in the fall of 1898. The effect of this, coupled with the judicious lumbering, has already become evident at the writing of this report. Small seedlings from last year's fruit are coming up in abundance in places where the conditions are favorable for germination. The seedlings are starting chiefly in the gutter roads, but the writer found many also coming up on mossy ground. On the heavy leaf litter no seedlings were found at all.

AMOUNT OF TIMBER REMOVED.

The following table shows the number of logs cut on Nehasane Park during the season 1898-99:

Operators.	Spruce.		Pine.		Balsam.		Cherry.	
	Number of pieces.	Standards.	Number of pieces.	Standards.	Number of pieces.	Standards.	Number of pieces.	Standards.
Contractors....	72,388	23,340.17	3,283	2,319.70				
Subcontractors	110,008	33,508.68	6,133	5,693,80	621	148.49	3	5.4
Total	182,396	56,948.85	9,416	8,013.50	621	148.49	3	5.4
Per acre on 4,331 acres...	42.1	13.15	2.2	1.9				

THE WHITNEY PRESERVE.

The plan of cutting adopted in the Whitney Preserve and in Nehasane Park were identical, but it was not possible to carry on the work of forestry as successfully during the first year on the former as on the latter. In order to understand the reasons for this it is necessary to know the circumstances under which the work was undertaken.

The lumber operations are carried on by P. Moynehan & Co., the partners of which company are Hon. W. C. Whitney, the owner of the land, and Mr. P. Moynehan, who has a certain interest in the softwood timber. According to the contract existing between the partners, Mr. Moynehan superintends the lumbering, receiving a share of the profits from the sale of the timber, and Mr. Whitney owns the land after the removal of the softwood trees. The first plan was to cut all Spruce measuring 8 inches or over in diameter at 3 feet from the ground. A clause, however, was inserted in the contract to the effect that Mr. Whitney could reserve all trees under 10 inches in diameter, but that Mr. Moynehan should be reimbursed at the rate of $1 per acre. As a result of a conference between Mr. Whitney and the Forester of the Department of Agriculture, it was decided to adopt the system of cutting used in Nehasane Park, namely, to remove all trees 10 inches and over in diameter, except those needed for seeding purposes, and to mark all trees which were to be cut. When this decision was reached the contracts had already been let for the season to lumber the Spruce to an 8-inch diameter limit. Four camps were in operation on and near Round Pond, one at the foot of Little Tupper Lake, two on Slim Pond, one near Mud Lake, and two on Forked Lake. The contract had been let for an additional camp on Forked Lake, but actual work was not begun until November. All of the contractors readily agreed to cut only the trees 10 inches and over in diameter instead of everything down to 8 inches, and to cut only trees which were marked. They were, however, unwilling to agree not to use Spruce for lumbering purposes, or otherwise to change the system of lumbering already used, except in the matter of cutting only marked trees for logs. The points in which the work of forestry was not successful are discussed under "The work of the contractors."

In accordance with the new plan of cutting the writer began marking timber on October 15, and within 10 days brought the work to such a stage that the lumbermen were cutting marked trees on all of the ten jobs in operation at the time. From six to eight woodsmen were employed to mark the timber.

The method of marking was the same as that described on page 71.

AREA CUT OVER AND THE EXTRA COST OF FORESTRY ABOVE ORDINARY LUMBERING.

The area lumbered over was 5,452 acres. As near as could be estimated, approximately 1,652 acres had been cut over before the marking began. The total area on which the timber was marked was about 4,000 acres, for there were fully 200 acres marked which were not lumbered. The total cost of marking was $598, or about 15 cents per acre.

The total number of trees left for seed over 10 inches in diameter amounted to 4,599, or something over 1 tree per acre. It is estimated that these trees averaged one-fourth standard each, making the yield for the entire 4,599 trees 1,150 standards. There were marked for removal altogether 282 trees under 10 inches in diameter. These trees averaged 0.22 standards each or the entire 282 trees 62 standards.

Under the new system of cutting Mr. Whitney paid Mr. Moynehan not only $1 per acre for the 8 and 9 inch trees left standing, but also a specified sum per standard for all trees 10 inches and over which were left for seed. The extra cost of forestry to Mr. Whitney was then for each acre lumbered 15 cents for marking the timber, plus the value of about one-fourth of one standard for each tree left for seed, plus the $1 referred to above.

WORK OF THE CONTRACTORS.

While some difficulty was found in compelling the contractors to cut only trees which were marked, the work was, for the most part, good, as far as the sawyers were concerned. According to the contract between Mr. Moynehan and Mr. Whitney the former was allowed to use any timber for lumbering purposes. There was, therefore, absolutely no check on the cutting of Spruce for skids, roads, bridges, etc. In consequence the work of forestry was, to a considerable extent, interfered with along the lumber roads, for frequently trees which had been

selected for seeding purposes were cut for skids, and a large amount
of young Spruce timber was cut for corduroy, leveling roads, bridges,
etc. (Pl. XX.) Back from the lumber roads, however, the forest was
left in excellent condition, and the difference in land lumbered before
and after the marking began was very noticeable.

AMOUNT OF TIMBER REMOVED.

The following table shows the number of logs cut on the Whitney
Preserve during the season 1898-99:

Locality.	Spruce.		Pine.	
	Number of pieces.	Standards.	Number of pieces.	Standards.
Little Forked Lake...............	49,016	13,962.55	4,141	3,420,63
Round Pond.....................	81,672	23,965.87	5,039	4,405.21
Slim Pond	70,344	21,310.94	4,870	3,982.61
Little Tupper Lake..............	43,323	12,757.56	4,858	3,910.32
Big Brook	22,384	7,319.07	1,548	1,246.80
Total	266,739	79,415.99	20,506	16,965.79
Per acre on 5,432 acres...........	48.9	14.6	3.8	3.1

THE SECOND YEAR'S WORK.

At the writing of this report the second year's lumbering had already
been begun both in Nehasane Park and in the Whitney Preserve, with
every indication that the work of forestry would meet with complete
success. The first year's work was unsatisfactory chiefly because the
lumbermen cut high stumps and wasted small Spruce in lumber operations. In order to remedy these faults the rules given below have been
adopted for the lumbering during the present season. A competent
inspector has been appointed for each tract to watch the work of the
lumbermen and to see that the regulations are complied with. Before
sending this report to the press the writer made an inspection of the
lumbering in Nehasane Park and found that the stumps were being cut
well within the limit given in Rule 5 and in many cases lower; that
practically no Spruce at all was being used in leveling roads; that no
Spruce was being used for skids except when really necessary, and that
in other respects the rules were being observed to the writer's entire
satisfaction.

RULES FOR LUMBERING DURING SEASON OF 1899.

(1) No trees shall be cut which are not marked.

(2) All trees marked shall be cut, unless a satisfactory reason can be
given for leaving them.

(3) No trees shall be left lodged in the woods, and none shall be overlooked by the skidders or teamsters.

FIG. 1.—WASTE IN LUMBERING: AN UNNECESSARILY HIGH STUMP; ALSO A SOUND LOG OVERLOOKED BY THE SKIDDERS. WHITNEY PRESERVE.

FIG. 2.—WASTE IN LUMBERING: SPRUCE CUT BY TEAMSTERS TO OBTAIN BRUSH TO CHECK SLEDS IN HAULING LOGS ON STEEP ROAD. WHITNEY PRESERVE.

(4) All merchantable logs must be utilized which are as large as 6 inches in diameter at the small end.

(5) No stumps shall be cut higher than 6 inches higher than the stump is wide, unless a satisfactory reason for cutting them higher can be given.

(6) No Spruce shall be used for bridges, corduroy, skids, slides, or for any purpose, except building camps, dams, or booms, unless it is absolutely necessary on account of lack of other timber.

(7) All merchantable Spruce used for skidways must be cut into logs and hauled out.

(8) Contractors must not do any unnecessary damage to young growth in lumbering, and if any is done they must discharge the men who do it.

APPENDIX.

[Compiled mainly from "The Adirondack Spruce."]

VOLUME TABLES.

Volume tables show the contents of standing timber. The primary object of the construction of such tables in the study of the Spruce in Nehasane Park was for use in working up the results of the 1,046 acre measurements taken in 1897, but it will be seen that they supply, in addition, the means of estimating standing timber with accuracy and dispatch, whether the result is desired in standards, board feet, cubic feet of merchantable timber, or in cords. They are based on measurements of the product of trees of different sizes actually cut in the woods.

Mention has already been made of the 2,006 stem analyses of small timber cut for pulp at Santa Clara, N. Y., and of the 298 analyses of trees cut into logs on the edge of Nehasane Park. The volume tables have been computed from the results of these stem analyses. Since this study is primarily for use in practical forestry, only tables of merchantable yield were made. For this purpose tables have been calculated which show the number of standards, board feet, merchantable cubic feet, and cords contained in trees of different heights and diameters.

VOLUME TABLE OF STANDARDS.

The number of standards in each tree was determined by Dimmick's rule, which is the common scale used in the Adirondacks. The trees were worked up together by grouping them in diameter classes differing by 1 inch and in height classes differing by 5 feet. It was found that the average results were so regular for the trees of different diameters and heights that it was possible to make a table by merely eliminating the irregularities by means of curves. At first the results of the trees cut for pulp at Santa Clara were kept separate from the results of the large trees cut in the park, but the two series were found to correspond so exactly that they were thrown together into the single table of standards given below. The diameters in this table are taken breast high, or 4½ feet from the ground. Lumbermen usually refer to the diameter inside the bark on the stump, but that is an unsatisfactory measure, since the height of the stump varies greatly. In dealing with standing timber measurements must be taken outside the bark. A comparison of the diameter inside the bark on the stump with the diameter breast high showed that, in the trees analyzed, the former was on the average three-quarters of an inch (exactly 0.79) larger than the diameter breast high.

79

I.—*Volume table for Spruce.*

Diameter breast high.	Height of the tree in feet.														
	25	30	35	40	45	50	55	60	65	70	75	80	85	90	95	100
	Contents of the stem in standards by Dimmick's rule.														
Ins.																
6	0.05	0.06	0.07	0.07	0.08	0.09	0.10	0.12	0.13							
7	.07	.09	.10	.11	.12	.14	.15	.17	.20	0.22						
8	.10	.12	.13	.15	.17	.19	.21	.23	.26	.30	0.34					
9	.13	.15	.17	.19	.21	.24	.27	.30	.34	.36	.42					
10	.....	.17	.20	.23	.26	.30	.34	.38	.42	.46	.50	0.54				
11	.....	.....	.22	.27	.31	.35	.40	.45	.50	.54	.58	.64				
12	.....	.....	.24	.30	.35	.40	.46	.52	.58	.63	.68	.74	0.80			
13	.....	.....	.....	.34	.40	.46	.53	.60	.66	.73	.80	.87	.94			
14	.....	.....	.....	.38	.44	.51	.59	.67	.75	.83	.91	.99	1.07			
15	.....	.....	.....	.....	.48	.56	.66	.75	.84	.93	1.02	1.11	1.22			
16	.....	.....	.....	.....	.62	.72	.82	.92	1.03	1.13	1.24	1.38	1.52			
17	.....	.....	.....	.....	.....	.79	.89	1.01	1.13	1.25	1.38	1.52	1.65			
18	.....	.....	.....	.....	.....	.....	.96	1.09	1.23	1.37	1.52	1.67	1.81	1.95		
19	.....	.....	.....	.....	.....	.....	.....	1.17	1.34	1.50	1.66	1.82	1.98	2.14		
20	.....	.....	.....	.....	.....	.....	.....	.....	1.47	1.63	1.80	1.97	2.15	2.33	2.51	
21	.....	.....	.....	.....	.....	.....	.....	.....	.....	1.76	1.95	2.14	2.33	2.52	2.71	
22	.....	.....	.....	.....	.....	.....	.....	.....	.....	1.90	2.10	2.31	2.51	2.71	2.91	
23	.....	.....	.....	.....	.....	.....	.....	.....	.....	.....	2.25	2.48	2.70	2.91	3.11	
24	.....	.....	.....	.....	.....	.....	.....	.....	.....	.....	2.65	2.89	3.12	3.32		

VOLUME TABLE OF BOARD FEET.

To construct this table the contents in board feet were determined for each of the 298 trees analyzed near Nehasane by means of the well-known Scribner's rule. The relation between the board feet and the standards was then found for each tree by dividing the number of board feet from Scribner's rule by the number of standards from Dimmick's rule. The average results for the different diameters, with the irregularities eliminated by means of curves, are given in the following:

Relation between board feet and standards in trees of different diameters.

Diameter breast high.	Number of board feet in one standard.	Diameter breast high.	Number of board feet in one standard.
Inches.		*Inches.*	
9	141	17	171
10	146	18	174
11	150	19	177
12	154	20	180
13	158	21	183
14	161	22	186
15	164	23	189
16	168	24	192

The table of standards was then converted into board feet by multiplying the number of standards of each diameter by the factor corresponding to that diameter in the above table. These factors do not correspond closely, except for the largest diameters, with those adopted by common practice in the Adirondacks. The latter range from 190 to 200 board feet to the standard. The present figures, however, are taken directly from the logs by the use of the two rules, and therefore show the actual relation between Scribner and Dimmick. Since Scribner undervalues small logs, such logs scaled in standards would also overrun these figures, because they are made directly from the rules.

II.— *Volume table for Spruce.*

Diameter breast high.	Height of the tree in feet.															
	25	30	35	40	45	50	55	60	65	70	75	80	85	90	95	100
	Contents of the stem in board feet by Scribner's rule.															
Ins.																
9	18	21	24	27	30	34	38	42	48	53	59					
10	....	25	29	34	38	44	50	55	61	67	73					
11			34	41	47	53	61	68	74	81	87	93				
12			39	48	56	63	72	81	88	97	105	114				
13					63	73	84	94	104	115	126	137	148			
14					71	82	96	108	121	134	147	160	172			
15					79	92	108	122	138	153	167	182	200			
16						102	121	137	155	173	190	208	232	255		
17							135	152	173	193	214	236	260	282		
18								167	190	214	238	264	290	315	339	
19									207	237	266	294	322	350	379	
20										265	294	324	355	387	419	452
21											322	357	392	426	461	496
22											353	390	430	467	504	541
23												425	469	510	550	588
24													509	555	600	637

VOLUME TABLE OF MERCHANTABLE CUBIC FEET.

This table was constructed for the purpose of computing the number of cords of pulp wood in trees of different diameters and heights. It was determined in the same manner as the table for standards, except that only trees which had been cut for pulp at Santa Clara were used. The merchantable cubic feet represent the amount of wood in each tree actually used for pulp.

III.— *Volume table for Spruce.*

Diameter breast high.	Height of the tree in feet.							
	25	30	35	40	45	50	55	60	65
	Merchantable cubic feet of pulp wood.								
Ins.									
5	1.1	1.2	1.3	1.4	1.5	1.6	1.7		
6	1.6	1.8	2.1	2.4	2.8	3.2	3.6	4.0	
7	2.1	2.5	3.0	3.6	4.2	4.8	5.4	6.0	6.6
8		3.1	3.9	4.8	5.6	6.5	7.3	8.0	8.8
9		3.8	4.9	5.9	6.9	8.0	9.0	9.9	11.0
10			6.0	7.2	8.4	9.6	10.9	12.2	13.5
11			7.1	8.6	10.1	11.6	13.1	14.6	16.1
12				10.0	11.7	13.5	15.2	17.0	18.8
13					13.4	15.4	17.3	19.4	21.5
14					15.1	17.3	19.5	21.8	24.2

In order to convert solid cubic feet into cords it is necessary first to divide by 128 the number of cubic feet in one cord, and then to divide by a factor which shall represent the relation between solid and stacked wood. In Germany this factor has been found from a large number of experiments to be 0.65 for round billets stacked in the woods. In consequence of irregularities in shape due to roughness of the bark and to swellings where the branches entered the trunk, this figure seems to give results too large for rossed billets. For the case in hand, 0.7 is more accurate. When the results of dividing the number of cubic feet (found in Table III) by the factor 0.7 are compared with those obtained by dividing the values in the table of standards by 2.92, which is the number of standards in one cord, determined by the Santa Clara Lumber Company from several thousand cord measurements, they are found to correspond almost exactly. After this confirmation of the factor 0.7, it was adopted, and the table of cords was constructed by dividing the values in the table for cubic feet by 128 and the result by 0.7.

IV.—*Volume table for Spruce.*

Diameter breast high.	Height of the tree in feet.								
	25	30	35	40	45	50	55	60	65
	Merchantable cords of pulp wood.								
Ins.									
5	0.012	0.013	0.014	0.015	0.017	0.018	0.019	....	....
6	.019	.020	.023	.026	.030	.035	.040	0.044	....
7	.023	.028	.033	.040	.047	.054	.060	.067	0.074
8	....	.035	.043	.051	.062	.072	.081	.090	.098
9	....	.042	.055	.066	.078	.089	.100	.110	.123
10	....	....	.067	.080	.094	.107	.122	.136	.150
11	....	....	.079	.096	.112	.128	.145	.163	.180
12	....	....	....	.111	.131	.150	.168	.190	.210
13	....	....	....	....	.140	.171	.193	.215	.240
14	....	....	....	....	.166	.193	.217	.242	.270

YIELD TABLES.

Present yield per acre of Spruce, amount which can be cut in 10, 20, and 30 years after lumbering, and the number of years which must elapse before the same amount can be obtained again, cutting down to 10, 12, and 14 inches, are shown in the following tables:

Yield of Spruce per acre 10 inches and over in diameter breast high.

Yield of all trees 10 inches and over in diameter breast high, in 1,000 feet B. M.	Number of acres.	Amount of first cut.		Second cut after 10 years.			Second cut after 20 years.			Second cut after 30 years.			Interval required between equal cuts, in years.
		Board feet.	Stand-ards.	Number of merchantable trees.	Board feet.	Stand-ards.	Number of merchantable trees.	Board feet.	Stand-ards.	Number of merchantable trees.	Board feet.	Stand-ards.	
1......	139	1,416	8.87	5.3	255	1.80	12.1	738	4.84	20.8	1,685	10.82	27
2......	213	2,382	14.47	5.4	323	2.34	12.8	868	5.84	21.1	1,991	12.94	34
3......	223	3,480	21.90	6.5	325	2.21	14.3	917	6.03	23.5	2,183	14.18	37
4......	204	4,228	25.74	7.5	375	2.55	15.7	1,070	7.14	25.9	2,420	15.57	39
5......	106	5,213	31.98	7.3	365	2.48	16.2	1,087	7.26	26.8	2,483	15.99	43
6......	71	6,005	37.32	8.8	440	2.99	18.5	1,581	8.40	30.4	2,913	18.80	43
7......	37	7,405	48.16	10.3	515	3.50	20.9	1,436	9.58	33.7	2,988	19.43	45
8......	21	7,868	47.78	9.4	517	3.57	19.2	1,366	9.18	32.1	2,899	18.95	47
9......	4	9,449	57.60	7.2	396	2.74	18.2	1,239	8.36	30.9	2,670	18.65	52
10......	5	10,499	60.92	8.6	473	3.27	17.0	1,043	7.18	29.6	2,938	17.20	51
11......	1	11,095	68.17	10.0	550	3.80	30.0	1,980	13.40	47.0	4,488	29.20	46
12......	2	11,772	73.19	13.0	715	4.94	26.5	1,887	13.67	46.0	4,542	29.41	48

Yield of Spruce per acre 12 inches and over in diameter breast high.

Yield of all trees 10 inches and over in diameter breast high, in 1,000 feet B. M.	Amount of first cut.		Second cut after 10 years.			Second cut after 20 years.			Second cut after 30 years.			Interval required between equal cuts, in years.
	Board feet.	Stand-ards.	Number of merchantable trees.	Board feet.	Stand-ards.	Number of merchantable trees.	Board feet.	Stand-ards.	Number of merchantable trees.	Board feet.	Stand-ards.	
1......	1,073	6.53	7.8	632	4.00	13.1	1,336	8.46	19.9	2,504	16.46	16
2......	1,927	11.80	9.1	845	5.68	14.5	1,560	10.21	21.9	2,995	18.20	23
3......	2,910	17.62	11.4	1,029	6.57	17.9	1,850	11.69	25.7	3,471	21.44	25
4......	3,608	21.52	12.4	1,131	7.22	19.9	2,115	13.47	28.1	3,924	24.23	29
5......	4,341	26.22	14.3	1,208	8.35	21.6	2,325	14.78	30.5	4,109	26.52	32
6......	5,153	31.43	15.5	1,412	9.01	24.3	2,686	17.10	34.0	4,778	29.49	32
7......	6,086	39.43	19.4	1,792	11.43	29.7	3,320	21.10	40.3	5,636	34.66	32
8......	6,933	41.32	17.0	1,696	10.97	26.4	3,019	19.19	36.2	5,264	32.44	37
9......	8,473	50.97	19.5	1,946	12.59	26.9	3,148	19.90	37.9	5,538	34.12	37
10......	9,155	54.52	16.8	1,711	11.03	25.4	2,964	18.80	33.8	5,283	33.73	40
11......	9,615	58.17	20.0	2,084	13.40	30.0	3,564	22.56	50.0	7,182	46.14	39
12......	9,800	60.14	29.0	2,957	19.97	42.0	4,739	31.41	55.5	8,767	53.80	32

Yield of Spruce per acre 14 inches and over in diameter breast high.

Yield of all trees 10 inches and over in diameter breast high, in 1,000 feet B. M.	Amount of first cut.		Second cut after 10 years.			Second cut after 20 years.			Second cut after 30 years.			Interval required between equal cuts, in years.
	Board feet.	Standards.	Number of merchantable trees.	Board feet.	Standards.	Number of merchantable trees.	Board feet.	Standards.	Number of merchantable trees.	Board feet.	Standards.	
1......	744	4.43	3.5	441	2.70	6.7	1,092	6.57	16.6	2.919	17.30	15
2......	1,425	8.48	6.2	990	6.22	10.0	1,864	11.36	20.7	4.041	24.27	15
3......	2,100	12.54	7.7	1,100	7.39	12.3	2,160	12.95	25.6	4.926	29.13	20
4......	2,840	16.53	9.4	1,339	8.23	14.9	2,624	15.09	29.3	5,810	34.35	21
5......	3,382	20.10	10.3	1,470	9.02	16.8	3,044	18.21	40.8	6,351	37.64	21
6......	4,035	24.06	11.7	1,646	10.68	18.5	3,369	20.14	36.0	7,531	43.92	22
7......	4,836	31.19	14.2	2,024	12.43	23.8	4,279	23.61	43.9	8,292	50.84	21
8......	5,380	31.46	13.5	2,043	12.55	20.9	4,095	24.47	39.9	8,378	49.82	23
9......	6,783	40.24	14.7	2,511	14.20	23.2	4,596	28.06	41.4	9,541	56.17	24
10......	7,835	45.82	15.2	2,465	15.25	23.8	4,769	26.52	40.6	9,349	55.02	27
11......	6,608	38.64	31.0	2,646	16.38	43.0	8,851	53.00	61.0	13,192	58.66	17
12......	7,072	42.16	31.0	5,047	30.31	46.0	9,381	56.01	73.0	17,409	102.10	15

ESTIMATE OF STANDING TIMBER IN NEHASANE PARK.

The table given below shows the estimate of merchantable timber on 1,046 selected acres, measured in Nehasane Park in connection with the study of the Adirondack Spruce by Gifford Pinchot. In taking the measurements all apparently sound trees were included. A considerable amount of timber will probably prove unsound when cut, and in order to obtain an accurate estimate, a certain percentage should be allowed for cull. In order to apply the tables to the entire area of Nehasane Park the following percentages should be deducted for unsoundness and for openings which may not have been included in taking the measurements: Spruce, 20 per cent; Hemlock, 30 per cent; Birch and Maple, 46 per cent.

Average yield per acre for merchantable species on 1,046 acres.

[Apparently sound trees without deduction for cull.]

Species.	Minimum diameter in inches.	All situations together. (Average of 1,046 acres.)			Swamp land. (Average of 225 acres.)			Spruce flat. (Average of 106 acres.)			Hardwood land. (Average of 442 acres.)			Spruce slope. (Average of 274 acres.)		
		Average number of trees.	Per cent of each species in merchantable crop.	Board feet.	Average number of trees.	Per cent of each species in merchantable crop.	Board feet.	Average number of trees.	Per cent of each species in merchantable crop.	Board feet.	Average number of trees.	Per cent of each species in merchantable crop.	Board feet.	Average number of trees.	Per cent of each species in merchantable crop.	Board feet.
Spruce ...	10	31.40	68.6	3,639	34.6	75.1	3,439	29.00	69.8	3,309	29.00	62.70	3,738	34.00	70.50	3,934
Birch	15	8.70	18.9	3,004	6.70	13.9	1,752	7.30	17.6	2,060	10.50	22.30	3,375	8.60	17.80	3,800
Maple	15	2.20	4.9	464	.60	1.3	116	.90	2.2	175	3.90	8.40	820	1.40	2.90	291
Hemlock..	12	3.30	7.2	982	3.00	6.7	1,150	4.10	9.9	1,151	29.00	6.30	839	4.00	8.30	1,008
Pine	12	.10	.2	74	.30	.7	99	.10	.2	83	.03	.06	5	.20	.40	160
Cherry ...	12	.06	.1	15	.04	.1	13	.04	.1	6	.10	.20	22	.04	.08	7
Ash	12	.10	.2	16	.40	.9	62	.08	.2	9	.02	.04	3	.01	.02	1
Cedar.....	12	.10	.2		.60	1.3										

BOTANICAL NAMES OF TREES USED IN BULLETIN.

Ash .... *Fraxinus nigra* Marsh.
Balsam .... *Abies balsamea* (Linn.) Mill.
Beech ....*Fagus latifolia* (Moenchh.) Lond.
Birch (Yellow) .... *Betula lutea* Michx. f.
Birch (White)...................... *Betula papyrifera* Marsh.
Cherry (Black) .... *Prunus serotina* Ehrh.
Cherry (Bird) .... *Prunus pennsylvanica* Linn.
Hemlock .... *Tsuga canadensis* (Linn.) Carr.
Maple (Hard) .... *Acer saccharum* Marsh.
Maple (Soft) .... *Acer rubrum* Linn.
Poplar .... *Populus tremuloides* Michx. and *P. grandi-*
                                    dentata Michx.
Pine (Norway) .... *Pinus resinosa* Ait.
Pine (White) .... *Pinus strobus* Linn.
Spruce (Black) .... *Picea mariana* (Mill.) B. S. P.
Spruce (Red)....................... *Picea rubra* (Poir) Diet.
Tamarack .... *Larix laricina* (Du Roi) Koch.